Illustrations and text by Gladys Perint Palmer

Assouline Publishing, Inc.
601 West 26th Street,
18th floor
New York, NY 10001, USA
Tel: 212 989-6810 Fax: 212 647-0005

www.assouline.com

ISBN: 2 84323 362 3

Color Separation by Gravor (SWITZERLAND)
Printed by Grafiche Milani (Italy)

GLADYS PERINT PALMER

FASHION PEOPLE

ASSOULINE

Although acute observation is a 'given' and passion is expected, humour is rare in art. We have to turn to the great political cartoonists such as Rowlandson, Gilray and Sem to find all three. They are the precursors of Gladys Perint Palmer's drawings, although she would add Lautrec, Modigliani and George Grosz—and I would not disagree. Such antecedents make clear what the pages of this book so admirably demonstrate: Gladys, whose work is always signed GPP, is not a painter but an illustrator of rare quality, possibly the last of a long and honoured line. Gladys has a highly idiosyncratic style—shrewd, detached and amused—based on an eye that has grown wise and sardonic with time. Early drawings produced for British *Vogue* in the late sixties were standard fashion illustrations, although even then, when she was still only in her twenties, a certain wayward wisp of a pen stroke and the controlled flourish of a brush mark were portents of things to come. Never interested in line-for-line reproduction of what she sees before her, Gladys soon learnt that capturing the character of a person or 'fixing' the personality of a garment was the result of a clear eye for detail, followed by the intellectual rigour to reduce all the information before her to a few telling lines. This is a skill all but lost today. Gladys is of the old school. She is a trained illustrator who spent three years at St. Martin's School of Art in London learning her trade, followed by time spent honing it at Parsons in New York. Since then she has drawn for some of the most luminous names in fashion including Missoni, Versace, Geoffrey Beene, Oscar de la Renta and John Galliano at Dior. Her work has appeared in *Harper's Bazaar*, *The New Yorker*, *The New York Times Magazine*, the *San Francisco Examiner* and the Style section of the *London Sunday Times*, to name merely a handful of her publications. She also worked with Robert Altman drawing on the set of *Prêt-à-Porter* which unfortunately turned out to be the world's worst fashion film, although GPP's drawings far transcend the travesty shown on screen. Born in Budapest, Gladys is a true daughter of an ancient country, turning her countrymen's passion and angst into a wryly humorous point of view. But the tenacity in her blood shows itself in all she does. I had seen and admired her work long before I found myself working with her on *The Sunday Times* Style section reporting from Paris on the fashion shows. It was an education on more levels than one.

Gladys does not have red hair for nothing, and for many of us it has been one of the great joys of fashion weeks to while away the stretching minutes, during which the great courtiers increasingly keep their audiences waiting, by watching her maneuvering to get the seat she wants, only too often sadly at variance with where the designer's PR representative wishes her to be seated. Adept and focused, cautious as a hunting cat, I'm pleased to say that Gladys gets her way rather more often than not. It tells us much about this highly talented woman. Gladys can be difficult, stubborn and rigidly uncompromising but the lunatic extravagancies of high fashion need a commentator such as she with an eye for affectation which is never blind to the skill and beauty inherent in the work of those other creators whose work she illustrates with such brio. And that is the point. Behind the dazzling display of technical panache in the drawings in this book lies the involved appreciation of human endeavour which all good artists possess. That is why Gladys Perint Palmer's unique work is so life-enhancing for us all.

Colin McDowell

1 DESIGNERS & GROUPIES

There was a time when a princess was dressed by a couturier and attended by courtiers. Today, the designer is often a prince who dresses merchants' wives. If he is a commoner, he hires a duchess to sell dresses and promote fragrances. Coco Chanel dallied with the Duke of Westminster but never married. "Everyone marries the Duke of Westminster," she said.

Titles who peddled clothes and class, past and present, include Emilio Pucci, Fiamma Di San Giuliani, daughter of the cobbler Ferragamo, Tai Missoni, son of a Serbian countess, Irene Galitzine, who invented Palazzo Pyjamas, Jacqueline de Ribes, Jean-Charles de Castelbajac, Hubert de Givenchy, Carolina Herrera, Diane von Furstenberg (the original Jewish princess), Simonetta de Cesaro (a thirties designer who left fashion to work in a leper colony), Lucien Murat, embroiderer, and the Duke of Verdura, jeweller.

Aristocrats in the fashion business include Amanda Harlech, Isabella Blow, Inès de la Fressange, Sibylle de Saint-Phalle, Loulou de la Falaise, Georgina Brandolini, and countless members of the Crespi family . . .

Fashion changed after Dior and Balenciaga. Before he retired, Cristobal Balenciaga said to Hubert de Givenchy, "You know, Hubert, life is changing. Customers do not need seven to ten suits each season, four or five coats and many cocktail dresses." He went on, "A suit is like a house. If it is not well constructed, the roof will fall in. The support of a garment is in the centre of the shoulder seam." John Fairchild has a different point of view, "The cut of a new jacket is not interesting. It's the drama around the jacket that matters."

In Paris, drama is global. It arrived from Germany with Karl Lagerfeld, one of three winners of the Wool Secretariat competition in 1954. Lagerfeld's judge, Pierre Balmain, promptly hired him as his assistant. Another winner, the 17-year-old Yves Saint Laurent was not so lucky. His judge, Hubert de Givenchy, refused to give him a job—but Dior came along soon after.

The night before the Chanel show, Karl Lagerfeld is at home, in his studio on the top floor of 31 rue Cambon, talking a mile a minute to his friends, in English, French, German, Italian about antiques, books, furniture, paintings, travel, and, at the same time, styling the show. Now he also has a publishing house and promotes a diet.

Drama came from Japan with the designers who deconstructed fashion in the early eighties. And with Brits, cockney and mock cockney. Captain Molyneux of Worth was the first to invade Paris. Today, Vivienne Westwood, John Galliano, Alexander McQueen, Philip Treacy, Stephen Jones, Stella McCartney, Hussein Chalayan, Suzanne Clements and Inacio Ribeiro challenge the old order.

A designer without a title —or a last name—needs a message. In June 1991, the art historian Federico Zeri announced that Valentino had invented the colour red.

TOUCHÉ! it is TEMPTING to IMAGINE rivals **TOM Ford** and **JOHN Galliano** STABBING each other in the FRONT. One can ONLY speculate **WHERE** their duelling BOSSES, **Domenico de SOLE** and BERNARD **Arnault** WOULD PLUNGE the blade.

On March 25, 1984, at 6:30 p.m. in the Jardin des Tuileries, **ROBERT ALTMAN** attended his first **SONIA RYKIEL'S** fashion show, fall collection. HE RESOLVED THAT DAY, to make a movie about PARIS FASHION. The 1995 film, PRÊT-À-PORTER was the result. SONIA NEVER LOST HER EQUILIBRIUM (L'Officiel, August, 1992).

REI KAWAKUBO of **Comme des Garçons** is the fashion Intellectuals' DARLING. At times she redesigns the body, adding a PROTUBERANCE where women would prefer to be CONCAVE

Still, she maintains a BALANCE.

ACCORDING TO HIS PARTNER, PIERRE BERGÉ, Yves Saint Laurent WAS BORN WITH A NERVOUS BREAKDOWN. In 1993: ELF/SANOFI BOUGHT THE COMPANY. THE DESIGNER TOLD BERGÉ: "you sold the company, YOU DESIGN the collection" and STAYED IN MOROCCO. In 1999, FRANÇOIS PINAULT BOUGHT YSL AND SOLD IT TO GUCCI. THAT WAS TOO MUCH. YSL CLOSED HIS DOORS IN 2002.

BACK TO MOROCCO!

Torchbearer,
CALVIN Klein,
Keeper of the
Eternal Flame,
passed to him
by YSL, Armani,
PRADA.... will
he ever pass
it on?

Fun and **GAMES** on the Roman Rings. High FLYERS **Domenico DOLCE** (cap) and **STEFANO** Gabbana cause a RIOT on the pavement of via S. DAMIANO, where **hundreds** of stiletto-heeled editors are herded before the collection. (L'Officiel, August, 1992)

At DIOR HAUTE COUTURE, GIANFRANCO FERRÉ ADMIRED LAURA JOHNSON'S **COCK.**

MRS. JOHNSON, OF PARIS, GENEVA AND NEW YORK DIED IN MAY 2002, HER **age still a SECRET.**

(Town + Country, September 1993)

STEPHEN JONES, HATTER TO JOHN GALLIANO and DIOR is bald as an EGG.
(S.F. Examiner, January 1986)

A **V**ery **L**arge **E**go

ANNA SUI, took GREAT offense at th drawing, part of a story about PEOPLE WHO ARE LARGER THAN LIFE. **Not just fat.** Her friend **Martine Sitbon** telephoned, outrag from PARIS. Then SUI's publicist phoned FROM NEW YORK, complaining. I asked, "ha he seen the story?" "No." "**Had Ms. Sui?**" "**NO**". **SO?** (L'Officiel, April/May 1993).

Is <u>LOUIS</u> <u>VUITTON</u>
<u>Malletier</u>, a bag or
a lot of baggage?
MARC Jacobs, who invented
Grunge, works hard to
make LV a fashion house.
Americans adore him.
Editors who receive <u>FREEBIE</u>
<u>LV</u> bags <u>WORSHIP</u> <u>HIM</u>.

Isaac MIZRAHI

American Renaissance Man?
or, WHY HE WENT OUT OF BUSINESS?

likes to sit in the **bath with a cigarette**, READING 'Memoires d'Hadrian' by Marguerite Yourcena

MEMOIRES
D'HADRIAN
MARGUERITE

DANIELLE STEEL, opposite, with daughters Victoria, Vanessa and Samantha Traina, at LACROIX Haute Couture, July 1999. They also shop at BALMAIN and DIOR

DONATELLA VERSACE watched her tiny daughter ALLEGRA BECK on the runway. In 1997, aged eleven, Allegra inherited 45% of VERSACE. Eating disorders followed.

Kingmaker Isabella Blow (never call her eccentric, you'll hurt her feelings) in **FULL GEISHA**, a nod to Alexander McQUEEN at Philip Treacy's show. London REPORT, FEBRUARY 1998.

YOU LOOK...
...WONDERFUL
SEASON BY SEASON
John Galliano
and Isabella
BLOW blossom
and flourish
and astonish.
March 2001

BERTY
PROW
PROD
PROWD
PRODUCT
PROUDA

SINK OR SWIM

Will PATRIZIO BERTELLI, on board the **PRADA** boat LUNA ROSSA – contender for the America's Cup in 2002/3 – throw a line to **Jil Sander**? Will **MIUCCIA** Prada notice? Will anyone care?

LUNA ROSSA

A!
ADA)

JIL
SANDER
SANDER
JIL
JIL

SOS!
HILFE!
HELP!

Donna KARAN vaults
OVER parallel bars AND
difficulties to please BOSS
Bernard ARNAULT

CLAUDE MONTANA DOES NOT ALWAYS VAULT OVER HIS DIFFICULTIES. (L'OFFICIEL, AUGUST 1992).

RITES OF SPRING 1993.
GIORGIO Armani invited
N'Dea Davenport, right,
Singer with the BRAND NEW
HEAVIES, AND Andrew Levy
also with BNH, to celebrate
the Emporio Armani
Collection.

"I'LL EAT my HAT if you don't get the job at Givenchy!" Isabella Blow might have said to Alexander McQUEEN at Christian Lacroix's October 1996 collection. Here with Katell le BOURHIS, now at LVMH, the former curator of the FASHION & TEXTILE Museum of the Louvre. (Punch, November, 1996).

FRANCO MOSCHINO AND HIS SILLY WIG IN MILAN MADE EVERYONE ELSE SEEM BORING.
AFTER HE DIED, IN 1994,
MILAN BECAME MORE BORING.
(S.F. EXAMINER, MARCH 1990).

THIERRY Mugler, playing himself, UNEARTHED many KINKY garments from long ago for his CAMEO Scene, March 7, 1994, in the Salle Gabriel at the Carrousel du LOUVRE.

Drawn for Robert Altman.

Curtains, left, at YVES SAINT LAURENT was always EMOTIONAL. Nan KEMPNER shed a tear. M. Saint Laurent STAGGERED or SWAGGERED, depending. Backstage, POLITICOS POSED, fashionistas fainted, groupies groped. (July 1999) LUCIE DE LA FALAISE, right, and her attendants stepped straight out of VELASQUEZ (L'Officiel, September 1990)

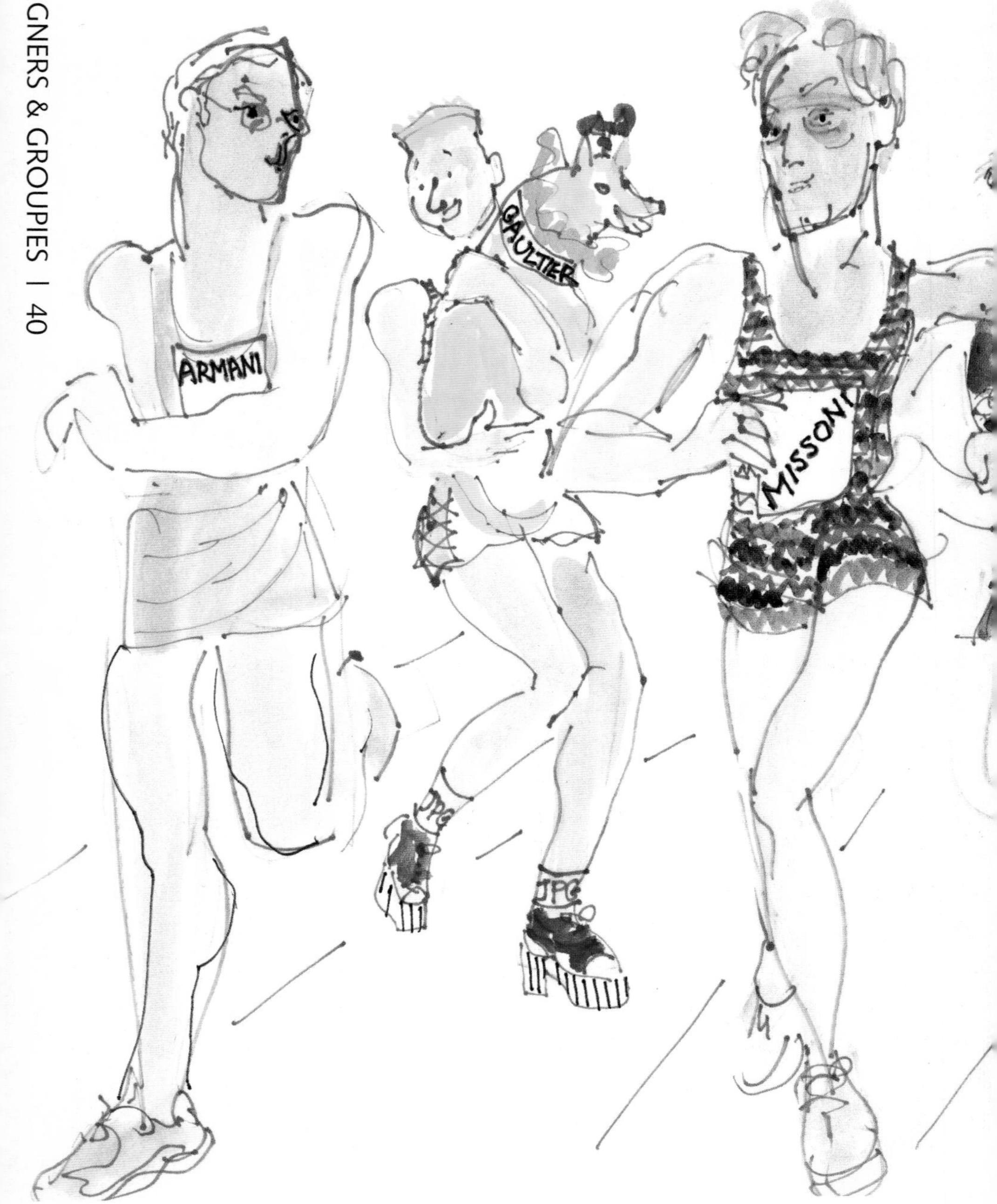
ARMANI
GAULTIER
MISSONI
JPG
JPG

SEE HOW THEY Run!

LACROIX

Giorgio ARMANI, JEAN Paul GAULTIER, with dog, Tai MISSONI (who won a gold medal in 1948 OLYMPIC Games in London), GIANNI Versace, CHRISTIAN Lacroix, and the winner was... ? (L'Officiel August 1992)

We THREE Kings from ORIENT are:

YOHJI YAMAMOTO, Rei Kawakubo, and ISSEY MIYAKE.

(L'Officiel, December, 1994)

Calvin KLEIN,
this page, and
RALPH Lauren
are the EMPERORS OF
New clothes. They are the...

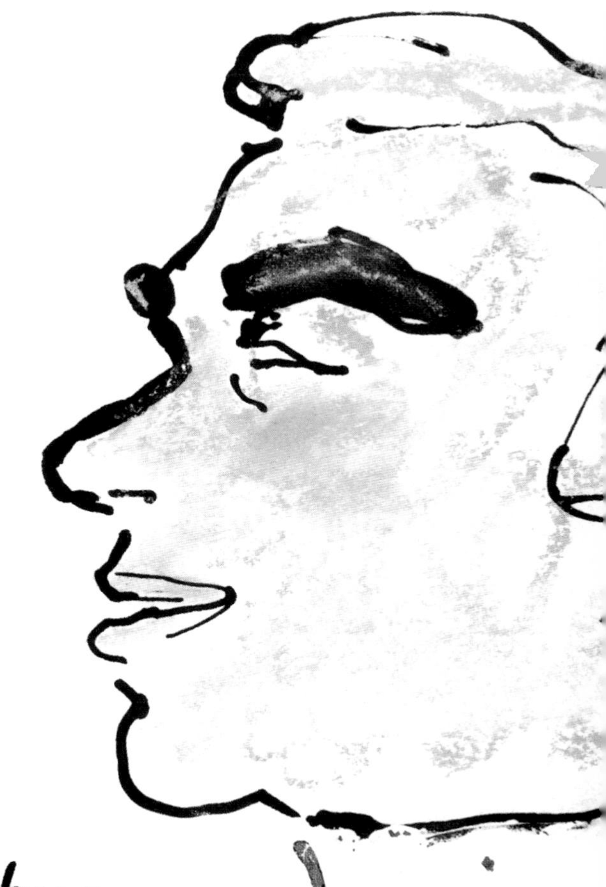

...Great Gatsbys of fashion. In a Calvin or a Ralph, you are an American Aristocrat – a MAYFLOWER Madam.

(Spanish Vogue, January, 1994)

A PRICKLY Pair
après moi la déluge
Gucci
TOM FORD
STELLA
LEE
YY
Comme çi Comme ça
LVMH
JOHN GALLIANO
ALEXANDER McQUEEN
JULIEN MACDONALD
PUFF DADDY
J.LO
FERGIE
CAMILLA
MADONNA
PHAT FARM
FAT CHANCE
VIVE LA FRANCE
why?
Yves Saint Laurent
Hubert de Givenchy

The two <u>MOST</u> **CUDDLY** designers in PARIS **AZZEDINE Alaïa** (<u>Arab</u>) and **Alber ELBaz**, (<u>Israeli</u>) should try their hand at (<u>re)dressing</u> the UNHOLY Land.

A few seasons ago, JEREMY
SCOTT, darling of PARIS,
PLAYBOY from TEXAS,
and KARL LAGERFELD'S
former friend,
EXPRESSED
himself.

"IT IS ONLY SHALLOW PEOPLE
WHO DO NOT JUDGE BY
APPEARANCE." (Oscar Wilde).
PAT FIELD the
neon - haired
costume mistress of
SEX AND THE CITY is welcome
at any fashion show Here, at UNGARO
in January 2001.
Pat

At a fitting BEFORE the October 1991 collection, Emanuel UNGARO RAMS a hat on a model "I'll MAKE it fit!" (Fashions of the Times, New York Times, February 1992)

LONDON Power!

Zandra RHODES, left, who lives in Del Mar, California, VIDAL Sassoon, who lives in Beverly Hills, California, and MARY QUANT, who stays at HOME

In SEPTEMBER 1992, I. Magnin had an Italian promotion, Bella Italia, in SAN FRANCISCO. They built an Italian city out of CARDBOARD. TAI and ROSITA MISSONI greeted the late Giovanna Ferragamo and her mother WANDA.

San Francisco designer KAISIK WONG (1950–1990)

was discovered by SALVADOR DALI in 1974.

In 2002 he was discovered by NICOLAS GHESQUIÈRE of Balenciaga

(San Francisco Examiner, August 1985)

NAPOLEON was a **Snob.**

He called the English a Nation of SHOPKEEPERS

An army of **French** SHOPKEEPERS all named GUERRAND-HERMÈS, DUMAS-HERMÈS or HERMÈS descended on San Francisco.

(San Francisco Examiner, December 1987)

I CARRY A FAN

I TALK TO FANS.
ONLY.

Condé Nast FANS — thick and thin
ANNA WINTOUR, thin, Karl LAGERFEL
not yet THIN (Paris, March 2000)

I CARRY A CROCODILE NOTEBOOK. ONLY.
I LIKE YOUR FLUFFY HAIR
SO IN VOGUE....

LUCIANO Benetton SURVEYS the world from Villa MINELLI, 200 miles east of Milan.
(S.F. Examiner, March 1989)

fashionfood: PASTAMAMA

During the month of October, Rosita MISSONI would rather be in the mountains, picking mushrooms. In MARCH, she is pleased to SERVE Italian food to the Japanese press (Milan, March 2000)

MASTER of the RING
Karl LAGERFELD pulls
NO punches.
Gianfranco Ferré
throws his **WEIGHT**
around (L'Officiel August 1992)

JOHN GALLIANO arrived in PARIS in 1990. He was asked, "WHY DO YOU DRESS WOMEN AS FUNDAMENTALIST FANATICS IN COCOONS?"

In 1993 he was hired by LVMH.
"WOMEN HAVE hidden behind BAGGY shapeless clothes for too long," he said
(L'Officiel, December 1993)

Elsa SCHIAPARELLI's SHOE is never OLD HAT!

(L'Officiel, December 1993)

EMANUEL UNGARO'S FANTASY: Toulouse Lautrec and to dress the Oldest PROFESSION (Mirabella, November 1989)

VALENTINO GARAVANI'S FANTASY:
Conquer PARIS with a little
help from JOSEF HOFFMAN
and the Viennese
SECESSION MOVEMENT
(Mirabella
November
1989)

GIANFRANCO FERRÉ'S
FANTASY:
Reborn CHRISTIAN
DIOR
(Mirabella, November 1989)

CHRISTIAN LACROIX'S FANTASY: THE BALLET RUSSE. (Mirabella, November 1989)

KARL LAGERFELD'S FANTASY: KAISER WITH A NEW KAISERIN EACH SEASON. (Mirabella, November, 1989)

MAD DOGS and English-men....

JOHN GALLIANO presented his July 1997 DIOR Haute Couture in a sweltering garden. **Stella** McCartney found a **FAN**, SYDNEY PICASSO found a **BOATER**, PATRICK Demarchelier found it **BLOODY** HOT. (Marie Claire, September 1997)

GUCCI NEEDS VIRGINS (Right). **Stella** McCartney and TOM FORD share a HOROSCOPE

GUCCI
TOM FORD
STELLA McCARTNEY

At NINA RICCI Couture, **CHANTAL CHAPIN**, the Best Client, arrived wearing a STRAPLESS SHORTS CONTRAPTION with Polka Dots, a CHERRY encrusted bolero, VELOUR watering-can bag, RED SHOES AND gloves. The VENDEUSES were fawning all over her.

Nowadays, <u>MADAME Chapin</u> is frequently sighted at **DIOR** and **Gaultier**, suitably dressed for her <u>age</u>.

Drawn for FASHION TELEVISION, July 1997

At Givenchy
Haute Couture,
there were **BIRDS**
of a **feather flocking**: pheasant
hat, ALEXANDER McQUEEN
with falcon, a GOLDEN EAGLE
SPLAT on Isabella BLOW's
head, black SWAN, TURKEY,
RAVEN. WHO needs clothes?
(Drawn for Fashion Television 1997).

SONIA RYKIEL'S BITTER CHOCOLATE PARTY AT

THE RITZ, MARCH 2000

THE INFANTA ELENA DE BORBÓN OF SPAIN WITH HER HUSBAND JAIME DE MARICHALAR, DUKE OF LUGO, GAZE AT CHRISTIAN LACROIX'S BRIDE AT THE JULY 1997 HAUTE COUTURE

2 FRONT ROW FACES

The front row at fashion shows is crammed with minor royals, film stars, café society, politicians and Madame Paul's graduates. No attempt is made to protect celebrities from the paparazzi; they are seated in the front row to be seen and to be abused by the press.

Celebrities are paid to attend shows, or they have something to promote. It is rumoured that Sophia Loren's price, just to show up, is $50,000. The big question, on January 19, 2002, was "How much did Donatella Versace pay Chelsea Clinton to sit in the front row?" A day or two later, when Chelsea had disappeared from the haute couture shows, the question was, "How much did Donatella pay Chelsea to stay away from the other collections?"

There is also the working front row. Merchants on one side, press on the other. A front row seat indicates not only placement but also position. You Are Important. You Have Arrived. You Matter. You Are Beautiful. You Are Clever. Everybody Loves You. Until you lose your job and can't get a seat.

Body language changes in the front row. An air of confidence settles on the occupants. When dressed in a short skirt, this relaxed posture can expose more than *Playboy*.

Publications fight bitterly for front row seats ("*Vogue* and *ELLE* have four! *Bazaar* only three?"). If seated next to a celebrity, even an anonymous Italian chanteuse, a front row seat can be hell. Hefty paparazzi charge to get their shot and trample anyone in the way. During one such riot in New York over Susan Sarandon, her children and her bodyguards, Anna Wintour of American *Vogue* took refuge in the fifth row.

It is important to learn the phrase,
"Le Premier Rang Surélevé",
the first raised row, usually the third or fourth,
where the view is better.
Yves Saint Laurent used to seat his mother
in the first raised row.

When the rows are not raised, it is another matter. From the second row, you can find a sliver of a view. From the third row you see only the heads in the first row. The fourth row is death. I have perfected the spot-and-sprint approach. Wait for the right moment, crouching, just before those with standing tickets are let in, then leap—vault, if you will—into the front row. Timing is everything. If you leap too soon, the rightful occupant of the seat may turn up (generally Marie-José Susskind of L'Officiel who is always late) and you have lost both your old seat and your new seat.

In July 1997, Gaultier gave me the back row. "Why?" I asked the publicist. I had assignments from *Talk* magazine, the UK *Sunday Times* and the *San Francisco Examiner Magazine*. "Because you always get into the front row and then you get in the video," he replied with fury. Clearly the poor fellow had been smarting about my orange jacket polluting the video for years. The following season, he gave me second row. Go figure.

ALL in short Skirts (from right to left): CAROLYNE Roehm, Isabelle d'ORNANO, Annette de la Renta, the late Pamela HARRIMAN, then American ambassador, Jayne WRIGHTSMAN

Oscar's mother-in-LAW, and SUSAN Gutfreund

at Balmain Haute Couture July 1993.

'Town + Country', September, 1993

"THE MOST INTOLERABLE PEOPLE ARE PROVINCIAL CELEBRITIES". (CHEKOV). Princess Gloria von **THURN und TAXIS** spent a King's ransom on Haute COUTURE and still looked **RIDICULOUS**. Then she had to SELL CASTLES, SILVER and PAINTINGS.

HERE at Thierry MUGLER'S Collection in 1986, She wore a JEAN PATOU hat, designed by CHRISTIAN LACROIX, with a RADIUS of five feet.

FRAN LEBOWITZ
at CALVIN Klein's show, October 1992
Later, TINA BROWN asked me to DRAW her for TALK, WHICH went SILENT before this drawing was published

BOB COLACELLO and Jaleh Taghari **MILLER**. In summer 1993, the couture houses received invitatio requests for a **MRS. MILLER**. Very excited, they ALLOCATED the BEST FRONT ROW seats. ALAS, Mrs. Miller, with a penchan for white LEATHER **hot pants** and GIANT papier MACHÉ millinery, was **NOT THE RIGHT Mrs. Miller**, she was a rep. for Jitrois leather in SAN FRANCISCO

MARIE-JOSÉ SUSSKIND (L'Officiel) and RURIKO HORIE (Marie Claire, Japon)

FIGHT OFF

Philip Treacy's KILLER ORCHID at Julien Macdonald's GIVENCHY Haute Couture, July, 2001.

IN the swimming pool of the RITZ – boarded over for the occasion – **Donatella VERSACE** launched her WINTER ATELIER COLLECTION under the scrutiny of **BOY George** with BLACK toenail polish and **MADONNA** WITH INGRID CASARES. Very large black bodyguards blocked the view of LESSER MORTALS. When the show was over, the largest bodyguard BARKED at little MADONNA, 'Walk! Walk! **WALK!**"

(Talk, October 1999)

PEDRO ALMODOVAR and JEAN PAUL **Gaultier's** favourite Spaniard, **ROSSY** de Palma, has ONE <u>dark</u> eye, ONE <u>pale</u> eye and ONE <u>**DROOPY**</u> eye She had a small part in ROBERT **ALTMAN'**s 1995 film 'Prêt-à-Porter'.

BOY George a Fashion Show FIXTURE since the eighties, <u>is known</u> for his flawless MAKEUP. He does a little **REPAIR** at Katharine HAMNETT's show.
(San Francisco Examiner, March 1987)

"SWANS HAVE AN AIR OF BEING PROUD STUPID AND MISCHIEVOUS – THREE QUALITIE THAT GO WELL TOGETHER." (Diderot).
OR, BIRD shit in the Front Row.
Mouna Al Ayoub's Philip Treacy HAT at John **Galliano's** show, March 2000.

Coronet and PLUMES at Guy Laroche —

and we
PUT IT ON
THE PRINCESS
of WALES

(L'Officiel, November 1993)

Autograph hunters BESIEGED CLAUDIA Schiffer and...

IVANA Trump after the
VERSACE
show in
October
1991.
NOTE
identical
BLONDE
bouffant hair,
pouting lips and
NEO CLASSICAL
Greek
SILK
prints.

LUCIEN FREUD likes to paint daughters and Kate Moss starkers. Turning the Tables, I drew him **NAKED** at Bella Freud's show, March 1997 for the Sunday Telegraph…

… and Bella bought the drawing.

On July 18, 1999, at **VALENTINO's** haute couture, **IVANA Trump** and **Betsey** BLOOMINGDALE, with **SERIOUS** PEARLS and a jewelled SPIDER. These fragile ladies have survived MARRIAGES, **scandals**,

REVERSALS of fortunes, even **monetary**, yet they are EVER READY to turn up at a **défilée**, and add snappy suits to their WARDROBE (Talk, October 1999)

POLLY MELLEN, winner of the 1993 CFDA LIFETIME ACHIEVEMENT AWARD, was bumped from the FRONT ROW at Sonia Rykiel's show on March 6, 1994, and stuck behind

SOPHIA LOREN, HER HAT AND

HER VEIL, and KIM BASINGER during the filming of Prêt-à-Porter in PARIS.

This drawing of
BROOKE ASTOR
when she
turned 95
was
commissioned
by TINA BROWN
who asked
that her wrinkles
be softened.
In 2002, Mrs. ASTOR
was one hundred
years old.
(New Yorker, April 21, 1997)

In July 1997,
Princess MARIE
CHANTAL of
GREECE attended
DIOR, BALMAIN,
VALENTINO and
CHANEL Haute
Couture
Collections.
SHE
DESERVED
A NAP.

In the place of honour,
at the head of the
runway at the July
1990 Haute Couture,
PRINCESS Caroline
of MONACO faced the
FIRING SQUAD of
photographers with
ROYAL SANGFROID.
(Mirabella, December, 1990)

THE DEEELite's **Lady Miss KIER** and SUPER DJ DMITRY (**where are they today?**) at MARTINE Sitbon's show. Lady Miss's blue Mugler cat-suit, fake blue fur and fake <u>RED</u> wig prompted the comment, **MISS'S <u>MISSES</u>.**

(L'Officiel, June, 1991)

SHARON STONE, DRESSED IN THE GAP, WON AN OSCAR ON MONDAY, MARCH 25 1996.

THE DAY BEFORE, WE PROPOSED HER AS **GILDA**

IN JEAN LOUIS' 1946 DUCHESSE SATIN AND MATCHING GLOVES.

(Los Angeles Times SUNDAY Magazine, March 24)

PRÊT-À-PORTER, the film: We raced to the Dior show on March 7. 1994. **Sophia LOREN** was wearing a RAVISHING hat. She had adopted **SALLY Kellerman** ("I'm her new best friend" said Sally) as a **SHIELD**. The press was FEROCIOUS.

After decades of PHOTOGRAPHING Madame Pompidou, MADAME CHIRAC, Sylvester **STALLONE** and obscure French nightclub SINGERS, the **FASHION PAPARAZZI** were in a **FRENZY**. Twenty minutes of SOPHIA/SALLY pictures followed....

A BED OF ROSES: The late Baroness Marie-Hélène de ROTHSCHILD, known for her Big Hats and Ruffles at the races, was ill for a long time. Her (hospital) bed was DAILY adorned with fresh FLOWERS and bows. She still loved going to fashion shows. Those who were invited STILL talk about her parties at CHÂTEAU de FERRIÈRES, twenty miles east of PARIS. No one mentions that HITLER had used the house...

"GOOD AMERICANS, WHEN THEY DIE, GO TO PARIS." (T.G. Appleton) Federated Department Stores' **BERNIE OZER** was **LARGER** than **LIFE** - when he was **ALIVE**. Known for his FEDORAS and PLUMES may he NEST IN PEACE. (San Francisco Examiner Magazine, July 2 1980)

At VERSACE, THE ARTIST, formerly known as Prince, his wife MAYTÉ, Puff Daddy, Anna WINTOUR, assist at the Atelier Collection, July 1999. (Talk, October 1999)

Hanae Mori's Haute Couture, July 1998 was attended by the artist CÉSAR and according to a vendeuse, a "MRS. BENNETT from somewhere else." Mrs. B. bore a STRIKING RESEMBLANCE to the wife of BABY DOC DUVALIER. Could SOMEWHERE ELSE have been Haiti?

When **Emanuel Ungaro** showed his January 1999 Haute Couture collection in the **PIGALLE**, his clients looked **somewhat** out of place after the show. **OR MAYBE NOT?**

At the Carrousel
du Louvre
in Paris,
March 2001,
seat CA2
was
reserved
for
MADAME
GISCHIA
an
ancient
ISSEY
MIYAKE
enthusiast.

New York and Paris fashionista, **MOKO**, <u>flows well</u> in <u>SUMMER</u> and WINTER. Here, at **JUNYA WATANABE** (March 2001) and at <u>KATOUSHA</u> at the BUDDHA <u>BAR</u> (October 1996)

TAKING **THE MICK.**
Princess Michael of Kent
("I never go to fashion shows"),

with **MICHAEL** Roberts
(New Yorker) and **MANOLO**
Blahnik at Philip
Treacy's 1997 show
(LONDON REPORT, February 1998)

OPRAH WINFREY IS
LARGER THAN LIFE
(L'Officiel April/May 1993).

PARIS **POWER** (the boys)
at Jean Paul Gaultier, July 2001:
Christophe GIRARD, Deputy Mayor
of PARIS in charge of culture,
Bertrand DELANOE, first GAY

MAYOR of PARIS and **DIDIER**
Grumbach, with the longest
title, Président, Fédération
Française de la Couture du
Prêt-à-Porter des Couturiers
et des Créateurs de Mode.

PARIS POWER (the blondes)
São SCHLUMBERGER, Claude POMPIDOU and Bernadette CHIRAC
at Valentino's Haute Couture
July 1993

(TOWN & COUNTRY, SEPTEMBER 1993)

PIERRE BERGÉ kept us on our TOES and told us when to SIT DOWN. He monitored the ballroom of the Inter-Continental Hotel where YSL showed his **haute couture** collections; and he STALKED the runway before the show started. THEN, he watched through a **PEEPHOLE.**

(L'Officiel, September 1990)

ANNA PIAGGI dressed here by Gaultier for the July 1991 DIOR collection at the PAVILLON d'ARMENOVILLE never disappoints. During a collection week in MILAN, her husband **ALFA** was undergoing a cataract operation. "Meet me in the hospital, we can have dinner." The hospital, on the **outskirts** of Milan, was a **bourgeois** establishment, with a surprisingly FINE RESTAURANT. Anna was waiting for me, wearing a **TUTU**, a MAD HAT, LEOPARD, LEGGINGS AND BONDAGE SHOES.

CHER at Chantal Thomass during the filming of Prêt-à-Porter, where she played <u>herself</u> — **who else?**

(JOYCE MAGAZINE AUTUMN 1994)

Armani was one of the **FIRST** designers to pepper his Front Row with <u>celebrities</u>. It is rumoured that Sophia **LOREN** charges $50,000 just to show up. Lesser celebs settle for clothes. **WHO KNOWS** what **ORNELLA MUTI**, left, and **Claudia Cardinale** cost?

Demi MOORE checks out GUCCI model's **bottom**.

(Grazia, January 1998)

PAUL BECK,
Gianni's model,
later Donatella's
husband, inspects
NAOMI CAMPBELL'S
bottom at the
Versace show
(Sunday Times
Style, October 19
1997)

DO BLONDES WITH STRAIGHT HAIR AND STRAIGHT TEETH HAVE MORE FUN?

ASK CHELSEA, GWYNETH, MADONNA AND DONATELLA

GEORGE LUCAS AND DAUGHTER KATY, AT THE PARIS RITZ IN JULY 1999 FOR THE VERSACE SHOW, WERE FAR FROM (THEIR SAN RAFAEL, CALIFORNIA) HOME.

"VULGAR OF MANNER, OVERFED, OVERDRESSED AND UNDERBRED." (B.R. Newton)

BUT when photographer EMERITUS Bill Cunningham documents your entry, YOU HAVE ARRIVED.
(CONNOISSEUR, AUGUST 1989)

Ashley JUDD, left, Princess Marie-Chantal of Greece, now wide awake and having a good gossip, and **Princess ROSARIO** of Bulgaria at VALENTINO's Haute Couture.
(SAN FRANCISCO EXAMINER MAGAZINE, DECEMBER 6, 1998)

Princess **FYRIAL** of JORDAN and Dominick Dunne at the July 1998 Valentino Haute COUTURE. The U.K. Sunday Times Style published ONLY fox and frock.

Inès de la FRESSANGE,
exiled CC princess
(POSING FOR THE STATUE
of MARIANNE was
deemed too BOURGEOIS)
with her daughter at
LACROIX HAUTE COUTURE
(Marie Claire, September 1997)

Hardly **anyone** recognized the usually GLAM Gwyneth **PALTROW** when she arrived at ALEXANDER McQUEEN'S **VOSS** collection in September 2001. **HE HAD sent** a Rolls Royce for her. She came in JEANS. **JONATHAN and RONNIE** Newhouse, who ATTEND more fashion shows than they eat **HOT DINNERS**, sat and waited.

At the March 1991 Chanel Collection, **OSCAR DE LA RENTA** and CAROLYNE ROEHM were seated in the Second Row (L'Officiel June 1991)

At the March 1991 Oscar de la Renta collection, film star **DOLPH LUNGREN**, famous for dating Grace JONES and for his role as the RUSSIAN BOXER who knocked out SYLVESTER STALLONE in **ROCKY IV**, was seated in the Second Row (L'Officiel, June 1991.)

ANNIE LENNOX of the
Eurythmics at one of
JOHN
GALLIANO's
earliest
LONDON
shows
from
the
last
CENTURY

MEN OF Fashion:
Vivienne Westwood
opened her
MARCH 1997
show with
a bare-chested
BAGPIPER
in a
lurex-shot
KILT and
Argyll socks.
He got a
STANDING
Ovation
also from
the STANDING
Section.

L'ENTENTE Cordiale: at OSCAR DE LA RENTA's Haute Couture collection for BALMAIN, Mrs. HENRY Kissinger and Madame VALÉRY Giscard d'Estaing expressed their THOUGHTS in BODY language.
(MARIE CLAIRE SEPTEMBER 1997)

Jocelyne Wildenstein and pompadoured paramour cum surgeon Svengali, **KEN GODT**, both veritable works-in-progress, attended Christian Lacroix's show in Paris on July 20, 1999.

There was **SPECULATION** that **MAYBE** her <u>hair</u> <u>was</u> <u>real</u>

(Talk, October 1999)

JEMIMA KHAN, wife of the cricketer IMRAN KHAN and daughter of the late JIMMY GOLDSMITH, sold her Pakistani embroideries during London Fashion Week 2000. Proceeds went to charity.

POWER **Sisters**, blonde pre-Raphaelites, **CARLA** and **Franca SOZZANI** control fashion in Italy.

Franca, left, is editor-in-chief of Italian **VOGUE**. Carla's shop **Corso Como** in Milan is de rigueur.

ON JULY 6, 1997, six days before he was

murdered, a blissfully **happy** **GIANNI VERSACE** showed his Atelier collection at the PARIS **RITZ**. It was a Celebrity Cleavage Contest between the catwalk and the Front Row, Demi Moore, left, Kate Capshaw (Mrs. Steven Spielberg), RITA Wilson (Mrs. Tom Hanks), Jessica Spielberg and Mimi Rogers (Ex-Mrs. Tom Cruise)

(DRAWN FOR FASHION TELEVISION 1997)

"CHARACTER IS WHAT YOU ARE IN THE DARK".
(Dwight L. Moody)

In recent times, KATE BETTS and JOAN BUCK got the BOOT at Harper's Bazaar (2001) and French Vogue (2000).

They'll be BACK.

FRONT ROW FROLICS AT DOLCE E GABBANA, MARCH 2002

LUCA

ANNA

GABRIELLA

KYLIE

MARINA

KYLIE MINOGUE and MARINA BERLUSCONI (daughter of the Italian Prime Minister)

FURTHER AWAY: LUCA STOPPINI and ANNA PIAGGI of VOGUE confer with GABRIELLA FORTE (ex Armani, ex Calvin Klein, now SUPREMO at Dolce e Gabbana)

In March 2002, STELLA greets fashion pop **SIR PAUL McCARTNEY** and bride-to-be HEATHER **Mills** – whose wedding dress was **NOT** by Stella.

In 1993, **JOAN COLLINS**, right, wore **DIOR TO CHANEL** and **GENNY TO YVES SAINT LAURENT.** Someone must have dropped a hint.

In January 1998, JOAN arrived at Valentino's dinner at Place Vendôme **IN VALENTINO.**

AT CHLOÉ, March 1999: MOUNIR MOUFARRIGÉ, managing director takes a **little nap**, and **CAMILLA PARKER BOWLES** is NOT AMUSED....

I CAN'T GET NO SATISFACTION
I WON'T FIND
NO PLASTIC SURGEON
Sir Mick Jagger
(at Julien Macdonald)
and Jeanne
MOREAU (at YSL's
farewell) HAVE
MERCIFULLY
RESISTED
FACE
LIFTS

MEN OF FASHION:

The Suits from the Stores at Fendi, March 2002.

There is a French proverb, "HE WHO CAN LICK, CAN BITE." Famous for his feuds, JOHN FAIRCHILD banned YSL from WWD in September 1987. Suddenly, they were BEST FRIENDS. Here is the reconcilliation with PIERRE BERGÉ.

Eleanor LAMBERT
98 years old
in 2002,
created the
BEST DRESSED
LIST
in 1940.
"There's
very
little
love
lost...."
(CFDA
Industry
Tribute
1993).

AT THE 1988
San Francisco Opera
opening, NAN KEMPNER
wore a **$1·5 MILLION**
necklace and **$500,000**
worth of rings and bracelets
by VAN CLEEF + ARPELS.
(San Francisco Examiner Magazine
October 1988)

POWER WOMEN – frequent and fervent front row occupants: **GRETCHEN LEACH**, right, wife of Howard Leach, the <u>American</u> <u>Ambassador</u> to <u>FRANCE</u> and **SYLVIA JAY**, wife of Sir Michael Jay, the former <u>British</u> <u>Ambassador</u>.

There was a row of Arab princesses sitting modestly at Christian Lacroix's July 1993 Haute Couture. Someone tried to SNAP THEIR PICTURE. Like a WELL REHEASED chorus, they picked up their magenta Lacroix programmes to hide their faces. (TOWN + COUNTRY, SEPTEMBER 1993)

Still GOING, going.... gone.
Queen of Fashion SUZY
MENKES of the International
Herald Tribune, left, Ellin
SALTZMAN, former fashion
director of MACY'S, and the
late CARRIE DONOVAN,
(New York Times, Old Navy) at the
HUBERT de GIVENCHY Haute
Couture, JULY 1991

Yves Saint LAURENT seated MADAME SAINT LAURENT, his mother, in the FOURTH RAISED ROW. He knew where she would have the BEST VIEW. (Marie Claire, September 1997).

Chignons at Yves Saint LAURENT: Irène Silvagni, director of YOHJI YAMAMOTO and a descendant of LEON TROTSKY, and

Carla BRUNI,
Socialite MODEL
at the July 1997
Haute
Couture

In the early Nineties, Madame la COMTESSE de Ribes, known as JACQUELINE to her American pals or MADAM RIBBS to Saks Fifth Avenue EXECUTIVES, was a designer, selling clothes and CLASS to SFA Customers. She attended MANY FASHION shows. (here at DIOR in July 1990). Her grand dinners on top of the Eiffel Tower, or at the Résidence MAXIM, or in her beautiful Hôtel Particulier on the rue de la Bienfaisance, drew princesses and film stars, politicians and press. We, the press, were seated separately to observe how the other side chewed. (L'Officiel, September 1990).

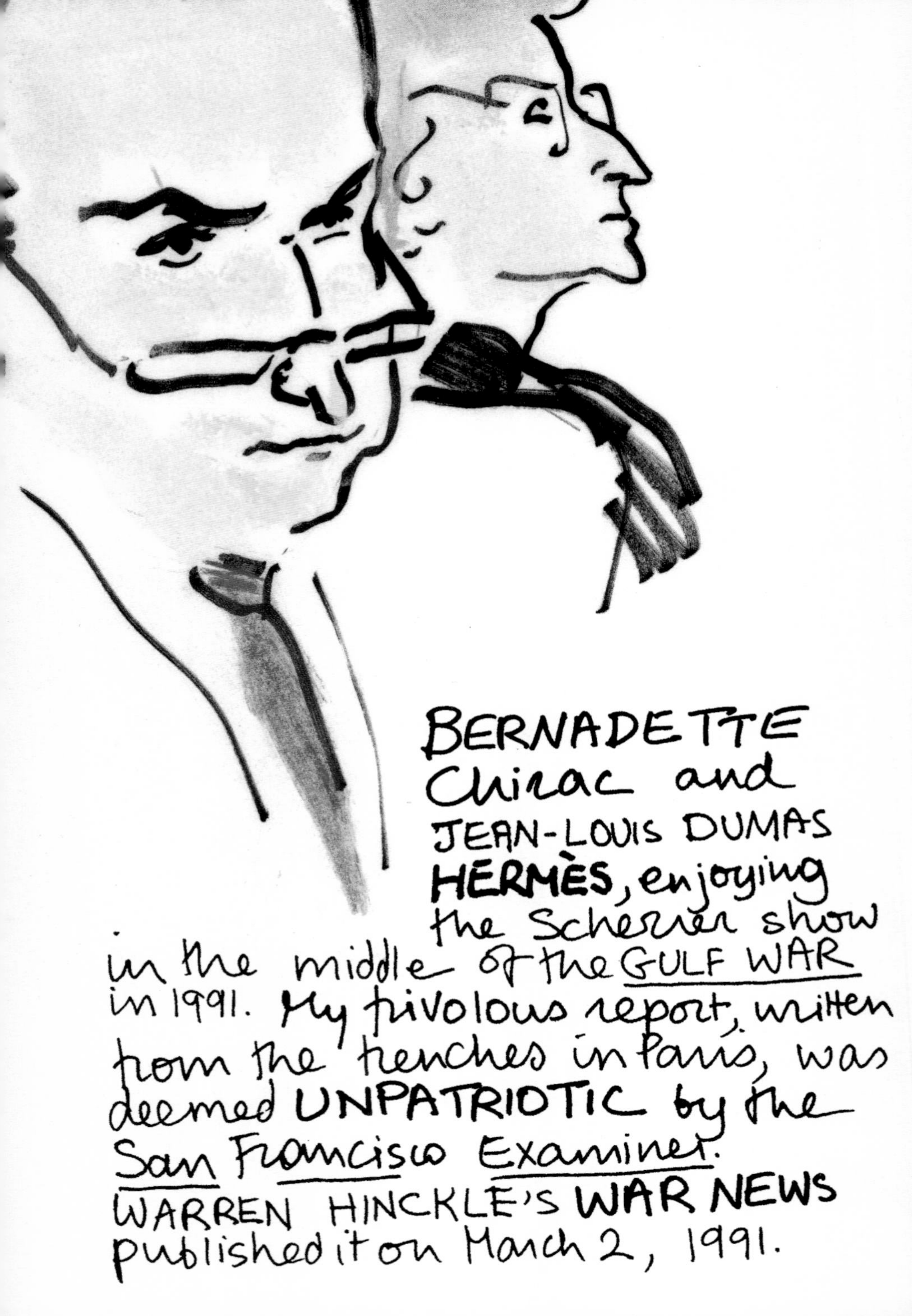
BERNADETTE
Chirac and
JEAN-LOUIS DUMAS
HERMÈS, enjoying
the Scherrer show
in the middle of the GULF WAR
in 1991. My frivolous report, written
from the trenches in Paris, was
deemed UNPATRIOTIC by the
San Francisco Examiner.
WARREN HINCKLE'S WAR NEWS
published it on March 2, 1991.

SIR HARDY AMIES wished
to acquire this drawing,
FRAMED. When told
it was for sale,
the answer was,
"SIR HARDY SAYS THAT
MUCH AS HE VALUES
HIS APPEARANCE,
HE DOES NOT
VALUE IT THAT
highly."
Sunday Times
Style,
July 11,
1999.

"A sweet disorder in the dress,
Kindles in clothes a wantonness."
(HERRICK)

ANNA PIAGGI OF ITALIAN VOGUE WAS A SPOILED DARLING OF A
ENAGE A TROIS...

PHOTOGRAPHER HUSBAND ALFA CASTALDI AND COSTUME GURU VERNE LAMBERT WERE DEVOTED TO DRESSING ANNA. NOW SHE IS TWICE WIDOWED. (N.Y. Times Magazine March 15 1992)

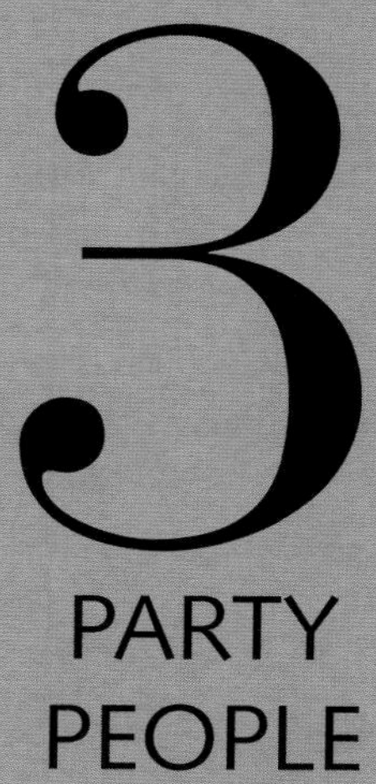

PARTY PEOPLE

There we were in Paris, January 1991, during a war centered around the very countries—Kuwait, Saudi Arabia and, to a lesser extent, the United States—that provided the customers for haute couture. Halfway through the collections we heard that Arab princesses, stuck in their native lands, were clamouring for the fashion videos, notably those of Louis Feraud and Jean-Louis Scherrer.

Party people never stop shopping. During collection week, Paris is perpetual commotion. It is a wonderful circus of freaks fuelled by insecurity which spreads like a virus. The cure is an endless preoccupation with fashion.

High fashion is perfect for flirting, it discourages passion and promotes safe sex. Many see it as a prickly armour or a jewel-encrusted bodyguard. Who can deal with fifty, tiny, slippery, satin-covered buttons down the back after a drunken party?

Fashion parties are also business. They provide opportunities to hobnob and kiss-kiss. The tier system separating the VIPs from IPs and mere Ps was demonstrated at an Yves Saint Laurent party at the Opéra Bastille. Everyone in the fashion business had been invited. Pierre Bergé, Yves, their close cronies (Catherine Deneuve, Zizi Jeanmaire, Maxime, Loulou and Lucie de la Falaise, Betty Catroux) and the truly elite media, merchants and clients were at a seated dinner on the top floor. One level below, the slightly less exalted were dining with YSL publicists and high-ranking executives. The unwashed press and minor YSL licensees were milling around in the lobby trying to snag a passing canapé.

Sit-down dinners are best but you may be stuck at the worst table. For networking, there are plenty of bun-fight buffets. To succeed, it is essential to arrive early and rush to secure the biggest table by draping scarves and bags over chairs. Then control who will sit with you. Make a rush for the food. Those who come later, or wait politely for the food frenzy to subside, will find themselves perching on a windowsill, juggling a glass, a plate, a napkin, cutlery and a handbag. Frequently the food supply has been much diminished.

In March 2002 there was a party, in honour of Miuccia Prada, at Azzedine Alaïa's breathtaking glass palace, 18 rue de la Verrerie in the quatrième arrondissement. We got there late in the evening, after the Alexander McQueen collection. Getting past the gate-crashers was a true challenge. Dozens clogged the narrow entry in the narrow street and argued with a solitary assistant holding a list of invited guests. Once inside, we gaped at the beautiful glass atrium, the palms, the subtle coloured lights. We circled and observed Ms. Prada and admired her necklace of diamonds as big as the Ritz. She was sitting at a table. All the other tables were occupied by people who had not bothered with McQueen. Perhaps they already had eaten. I saw a few trays of canapés, all identical.

I said hello to a few people
but if they said hello back,
I couldn't hear.
Nobody asked me to dance.
I went home rather hungry.

BONJOUR M. TALL
ANDRÉ
ANDRÉ
HELLO LITTLE PEOPLE
POOR BUNNY
ANTI FUR

"IMITATION IS THE SINCEREST FORM OF FLATTERY." (C.C. COLTON)
André LEON TALLEY, 6'7", makes an ENTRANCE in **FUR** (MARCH 2000)

"IMITATION IS SUICIDE." (EMERSON). Another of Karl LAGERFELD's discarded muses, Princess DIANE de Beauvau Craon. WHEN IN favour, she dressed in UNIFORM: parking attendant, policeman, SECURITY guard. HERE at FENDI, she is an Italian police officer. (San Francisco EXAMINER, MARCH 1990)

IN the hallway of
THE CARROUSEL DU LOUVRE,
March 2001,
AMANDA
Lepore
wore a
SEE-THROUGH
SPLIT
SHREDDED
Sheath,
Scattered
with SEQUINS,
armed with furs,
escorted by
DAVID LaChapelle.
EVEN fashionistas STARED.

JULIA ROBERTS played the fashion
editor of the HOUSTON CHRONICLE

and TRACY ULLMAN in Philip Treacy, played the editor of BRITISH VOGUE in PRÊT-À-PORTER, 1994

SYLVESTER STALLONE AND ANDRÉ LEON TALLEY IN PINK SHANTUNG THREE PIECE SUIT AT GAULTIER.

'L'OFFICIEL JUNE 1991)

In MARCH 2000, the **MISS RODEO CUM WILD WEST CUM RALPH LAUREN** book party at the terminally chic

boutique, COLLETTE, in Paris had everyone asking, "**WHAT WAS ALL THAT ABOUT?**"

THIS DRAWING for the DIANA VREELAND retrospective at the MET. WAS COMMISSIONED by VALENTINO Garavani in October 1993. I had to illustrate a dinner at MRS. VREELAND'S house for Jackie O. and Barbra STREISAND.

Sophia LOREN
had flown back
to Italy "BUT HER
SPIRIT WAS THERE." So I
put Sophia in the CURTAINS.

QUENTIN Crisp was a FLAMBOYANT FASHIONISTA. He'll meet MANY in HEAVEN. MORE in HELL.

Lyle LOVETT, then Julia ROBERTS' husband PLAYED A TEXAS BOOT MOGUL in *Prêt-à-Porter*. HE WORE his own ALLIGATOR BOOTS, much envied by the Cast...

"Draw a mis-en-scène, Gladys," suggested Colin McDowell to illustrate his March 1998 PARIS report for Sunday Times Style. I drew John Galliano's kinky boys and girls circa Thirties Berlin.

LEFT: In Paris during **fashion week**, clients BRAG about bodyguards and **COMPLAIN** about the **French**. **CELINE DION** had a huge protector at [Chanel logo] in March 1998.

ABOVE: "I HAVE NOT YET BEGUN TO FIGHT." (John Paul Jones).

MADONNA's bodyguard even followed her ON THE RUNWAY at **Dolce e Gabbana** (GRAZIA, NOVEMBER 22, 1992)

Dress in San Francisco can be VERY FANCY
Ann Getty wears C, DIOR. Fitters fly in from PARIS....
NOT TO BE outdone, GORDON GETTY dressed up as MARCO POLO
(San Francisco Examiner Magazine February 12, 1989).

ANNA Piaggi wore ROMEO GIGLI's cotton velvet coat, WITH RICH BYZANTINE embroidery from the Fall 1989 Collection (retail $38,000 to ordinary MORTALS)

(ELLE U.K. July 1991.)

TH**IN** **MEN**: inspired perhaps by DIOR MEN'S DESIGNER HEDI **SLIM**ANE, KARL LAGERFELD HAS BECOME WAFER THIN.

OTHERS EQUALLY ONE DIMENSIONAL: LIONEL VERMEIL AND RICHARD BUCKLEY.

"NO ONE HATES HIS BODY."
(Saint Augustine)
BUT Maybe Karl Lagerfeld can help MARIANNE FAITHFULL
at
October 1999.

Left: L'enfant Terrible, JEAN PAUL GAULTIER, turned fifty in 2002. THIS EARLIER, NUTTIER finale, FALL/WINTER 1992/3, complete with BUSKERS, LAVATORY PAPER ROLLS, ARTICULATED SHAVING MIRRORS, **CAMERA HATS** AND more, was used on the JANUARY 2001 cover of the magazine, JAPANESE TRENDSETTER

Above: **It's ALL PERCEPTION**: In March, 2000, ANGELA Missoni created a floral BACKDROP of **TULIPS**, held ALOFT backstage by an assistant WITH TIRED ARMS.

MARGARET Thatcher, **BEST** Dressed, in AQUASCUTUM, is <u>REALITY</u>.
(Connoisseur, August 1989)

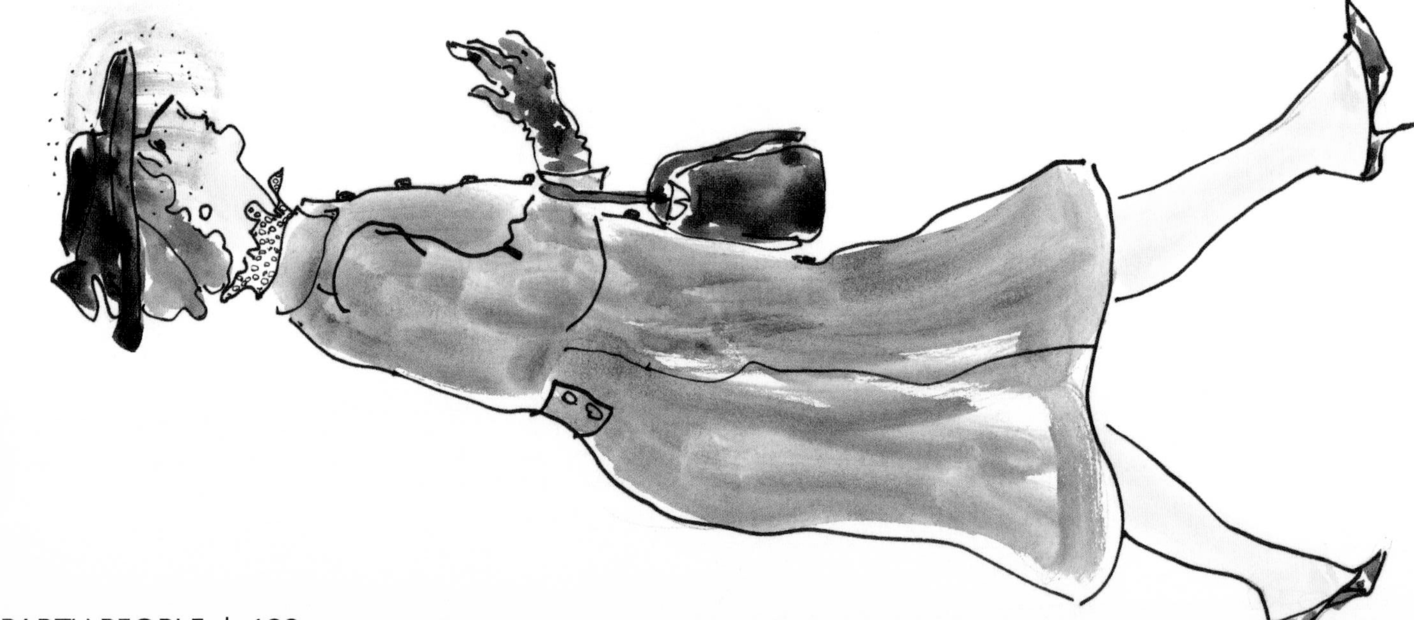

Margaret THATCHER, **LESS** *dressed*, is <u>fantasy</u>. (Mirabella, September, 1989)

Versailles party, July 1999, was a TOUR DE FORCE.... After the **DIOR** SHOW in L'ORANGERIE, a sunset buffet WITH **BALLOONS** UNDER Palm TREES for, (left to right:) **gender-BENDER** model who opened the SHOW ("did you KNOW whether I was a BOY OR A GIRL?")

Also present, Eloisa BERCERO an ancient COUTURE CLIENT from SPAIN, and HÉLÈNE and BERNARD ARNAULT – who owns LVMH. (Isabella Blow had her handbag stolen...)

CELEBRITY TIME IN PARIS:
Thierry Mugler created this
EDWARDIAN EXCESS for
CLUB QUEEN
DIANNE BRILL

CELEBRITY TIME IN NEW YORK: Prima Donna **JESSYE NORMAN** was often sighted at **BILL BLASS**

HARVEY WEINSTEIN (**The Suit**) AND RICHARD GLADSTEIN (**The Sweater**) CAME TO PARIS IN 1994 DURING THE FILMING OF PRÊT-À-PORTER.

<u>EVERYONE</u> LOVED HARVEY. HE <u>LOATHED</u> THIS DRAWING.

OPPOSITE: THOSE WHO SAT <u>NEAR</u> **Sylvester Stallone** AT VERSACE SWORE HE KNEW ONLY <u>FOUR</u>-<u>LETTER</u> <u>WORDS</u>. (L'Officiel, September 1991).

In the early Nineties, it was hard to tell who was a
MODEL,
who was an
AGENT,
who was a
GROUPIE,
who was a
PIMP.
THEY ALL LOOKED
CHIC.

Actor RUPERT EVERETT modelled for YSL.
In Prêt-à-Porter he was strictly SAVILLE ROW.
A PIN STRIPE PIN UP

Philip Treacy made me a HAT for my son's wedding in 1996. HE MADE A HAT FOR MY MOTHER. TO accomodate THREE PEOPLE, THREE SUITCASES AND TWO HAT BOXES, we had to hire the biggest car at Boston airport.

Harry Belafonte, dressed from top to toe in (<u>his</u> <u>own</u>) Armani, had a cameo role in PRÊT-À-PORTER.

He spilt soup on his tie

and brought the <u>FILMING</u> <u>TO</u> <u>A</u> <u>HALT</u>.

The costume mistresses were running around looking for a <u>SPOT</u> <u>REMOVER</u>....

OSCAR

Designer **ZANDRA RHODES** can SLEEP <u>anywhere</u>.

In March 1997, jet-lagged, she settled on the pavement WHILE WAITING for her **STRETCH limousine** after the Oscars.

TIM Robbins, right, was LESS RELAXED about his lost limo.

When life was rosy.
Sir Elton John with
pink SPECTACLES and
gold button earrings
at the VERSACE Atelier
Collection in July 1993.
(Town and Country, September 1993)

Beauty in the eye of the **beholder**. At **GIVENCHY** Haute Couture, July 1991, **ESTÉE LAUDER** wears psychedelic sun**glasses**

At YVES SAINT LAURENT Haute Couture, on July 21, 1991, Catherine DENEUVE, friend, film star and spokeswoman for YSL PRODUCTS, offers an **unbiased** opinion to ALBER ELBAZ and JEAN PAUL GAULTIER.

ZIZI Jeanmaire heard it all BEFORE

DON'T ask. Don't be fooled. These ARAB BUYERS (at Ferré, Krizia and Fendi) dress to the NINES when there are no MEN around. Furthermore, their CUSTOMERS pay **full price** and order styles by the DOZEN A single Saudi Royal Wedding can keep a minor couture house afloat **FOR A YEAR**.

The beautiful **PAT** Cleveland, one of **ANTONIO'S GIRLS**, wept buckets during Thierry Mugler's collection in MARCH 1987. She had just heard that ANTONIO had **DIED in California**. And she was wearing **WEEDS**

On JULY 17, 1999,
Donatella Versace
gave a dinner
under giant

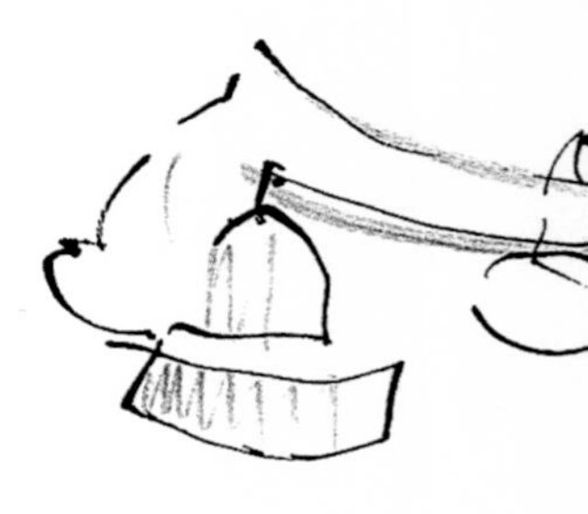

Sexy PLASTER
GODDESSES,
bamboo
lanterns
and
assorted
ASIAN
artifacts
at the
RESTAURANT
MAN RAY – the IN place
to eat DINNER but
NOT LUNCH.

BELOW: Model waits for the **SIXTH** television interview to be over to say GOODBYE to **Alexander McQUEEN** after the GIVENCHY Haute Couture, July 1997. (Marie Claire, September 1997)

OPPOSITE: Some may recall the CONNECTION between **MARIANNE** Faithfull and **JADE JAGGER**. It is sad to see where too many **MARS BARS** can settle – in Lainey KEOGH's pink whaleboned corset. (San Franciso Examiner Magazine, November 23, 1997)

THANK HEAVEN FOR little girls. JOHN Galliano, left, changes his costume EVERY season. In January 1999, at the DIOR Haute Couture, he looked like Maurice Chevalier and made a little speech.

POP STAR? Camilla Morton, editor-at-large and John Galliano's BEST FRIEND, was asked TWO NIGHTS before Galliano's show in October 2001, HOW IT WAS GOING. "SO far," she attested, "he's got LEG WARMERS."

PHOTO OP PAR EXCELLENCE
Vanessa Getty, Michael KORS,
and Tatianna Sorokko after Celine, October 2000.

WINNER OF THE 2002 PALME D'OR, **ROMAN Polanski** and a very possessive EMMANUELLE SEIGNER <u>his</u> <u>WIFE</u>, at the Versace Atelier Collection, in July 1993.

DODIE Rosekrans, CHEVALIER DES ARTS ET DES LETTRES, was one of **John Galliano's** backers. Known for her splendid residences in **VENICE** and **PARIS**, She wears DIOR, GALLIANO and GAULTIER. Here, dressed in Galliano, she stands on a CARVED LIMESTONE balcony under the atrium of her palazzo, WHICH for FORTY YEARS was the residence of the Archbishops of San Francisco. WHEN THE LAST archbishop took a VOW OF **POVERTY** in 1980 and moved to a NUNNERY, it was sold to the late JOHN N. ROSEKRANS JR.

Tatiana SOROKKO bundled all her **MINK**-clad friends, **RUSSIAN** and otherwise, into a taxi and headed straight for the **SALLE WAGRAM** for FRÉDÉRIC MOLENAC'S spring 2002 haute couture collection. ALAS, Frédéric was experiencing a **FASHION MOMENT** and refused to talk to anyone afterwards.

THIS PAGE: ANTI-FASHION STATEMENT AT ISAAC MIZRAHI'S MARCH 1995 SHOW BY **Sandra Bernhard**, left, **Roseanne Arnold** and **Liza Minelli** (BURDA, WINTER 1995/6)

OPPOSITE: Model **Susie Bick** and husband **Nick Cave** (lead singer of THE BAD SEEDS) at PHILIP TREACY'S WILD 2000 Show at Tiffany's, Bond Street, with Ferraris, Lamborghinis, Rolls Royces, and hats on bonnets.

PALOMA PICASSO
travels.
"I always know which country I am in. They pronounce my name differently.
PAL-OH-MA in America.
PALO-MAA in France.
PAAH-LOMA in Spain."
The ART WORLD is CRITICAL:
"Paloma is SO CHIC, she is a traitor!" (San Francisco Examiner 1986)

"EVERYBODY WANTS TO BE SOMEBODY; NOBODY WANTS TO GROW." (Goethe).

Sitting at the *head* of the runway at the JULY 1993 Haute Couture, Richard GERE, left, *winked* at his (then) *wife* CINDY Crawford.

Prince ALBERT of Monaco sat to the side and chewed GUM, ignoring CLAUDIA Schiffer. (Town and Country, September 1993.)

Changing of the GUARD at LANVIN 2002; the new majority owner, from TAIWAN, MADAME WONG SHIAO LAN might have met Maryll Lanvin, the designer from 1982-1989 at a fashion show in PARIS. Then again, maybe not.

HERE IS THE KEY PHRASE TO USE ON A P.R. (ASSUMING SHE IS NOT HAVING LUNCH, TEA, COFFEE, OR IS OUT, OR DEAD): "MON INVITATION N'EST PAS ARRIVÉE... !" IT WON'T HELP.

HIDDEN ASSETS: ONE IMPORTANT P.R. IN PARIS IS A CHRISTIAN SCIENTIST; ANOTHER, A SCIENTOLOGIST; ANOTHER VITAL PLAYER VISITS ASHRAMS IN INDIA AND UPPER NEW YORK STATE. CONTEMPLATE IT.... AND LEARN **Ommmmmm** AND **Aaaaah**. <u>AND</u> <u>BREATHE</u>.

A PAIR OF EARPLUGS IS FAR MORE VALUABLE THAN A PAIR OF <u>MANOLOS</u>. THEY WILL HELP YOU SURVIVE HUMDRUM COLLECTIONS THAT FEATURE A HUNDRED AFRICAN **DRUMMERS** AND TWO HUNDRED DECIBELS — NEXT SEASON WHEN YOU GET INTO THE SHOWS.

THE SHOWS:

NEXT TIME AROUND, MAYBE YOU WILL BE INVITED TO ONE (OR TWO) MINOR FASHION SHOWS. YOUR **SEAT** WILL BE **STANDING** AND YOUR VIEW OF THE CATWALK AS ILLUSTRATED

A FEW YEARS LATER

IF YOU REALLY PERSIST, YOU MAY GET A SEAT— IN THE BACK ROW. YOUR VIEW WILL BE AS ABOVE

IF YOU WANT TO UPGRADE YOUR SEAT TO ROWS 2-3, YOU MUST NEVER SAY ANYTHING MORE NEGATIVE THAN "IT WAS **INTERESTING.**" YOU MUST RAVE, RAVE AND RAVE, POSSIBLY IN PRINT AND SEND CLIPPINGS TO P.R.s AND TALK ABOUT YOURSLEF AD NAUSEUM

WHEN –IF– YOU ARRIVE IN THE **FRONT ROW** YOU MUST NEVER SPEAK TO ANYONE WHO IS **NOT IN THE FRONT ROW** BUT REMEMBER, THOSE BEHIND YOU ARE LISTENING, SO TALK ABOUT THE GORGEOUS FLOWERS/FRUIT/GIFTS EACH DESIGNER SENT YOU AND **WHICH PARTY** YOU WILL ATTEND TONIGHT (OUT OF FOUR).

PROTOCOL:

LEARN TO KISS EVERYONE ON BOTH CHEEKS. CALL EVERYONE **DARLING**. NEVER TURN YOUR BACK (IF YOU WANT TO SURVIVE.)

GO BACKSTAGE AFTER COLLECTIONS AND KISS THE DESIGNERS ON BOTH CHEEKS, CALL THEM <u>DARLING</u>, TELL THEM HOW FABULOUSLY SLIM THEY LOOK AND ASK FOR THEIR DIET DOCTOR AND NEVER TURN YOUR BACK.

"WHEN WOMEN KISS, IT ALWAYS REMINDS ME OF PRIZEFIGHTERS SHAKING HANDS," SAID MENCKEN.

ANYONE YOU HAVE NOT SEEN FOR 24 HOURS MUST BÉ KISSED ON BOTH CHEEKS. <u>AGAIN</u>.

AFTER THE KISSES, SHUT UP ABOUT YOUR <u>FLU</u>/<u>UPSET STOMACH</u>/<u>BUNIONS</u>

ESPECIALLY IF THEY ARE INFECTIOUS OR CONTAGIOUS. YOU WILL BE TREATED LIKE A LEPER. OR WORSE.

GET NOTICED:

WEAR A COSTUME FESTOONED WITH FLORA AND FAUNA (STUFFED AND ALIVE). GET A SMALL DOG. TIE A LITTLE BOW. LET HIM RUN AROUND. LEAVE HIM IN THE LIMO. (EVERYONE WILL KNOW YOU HAVE A WARM HEART AND A LIMO).

ARRIVE WITH A VERY LARGE
Escort in Ethnic
garb, or a STAR
PHOTOGRAPHER:

WEAR 8 INCH STILETTOS OR BONDAGE SHOES; PEARLS, DIAMONDS, ANIMAL PRINTS AND EYE CONTACT OPTIONAL.

YOUR LIMO MUST BE PARKED AS CLOSE TO THE FASHION SHOWS AS

POSSIBLE AND ENTIRELY BLOCK PEDESTRIAN ACCESS. SMOKE ANYWHERE YOU WANT. THOSE <u>**DÉFENDU**</u> AND <u>**INTERDIT**</u> SIGNS ARE FOR FOLKS WITHOUT A LIMO.

MODEL MOMENTS

*Models are freaks of nature.
Ridiculously thin and gorgeous.
They tower over normal people, they are under
the age of consent and too young to vote.
Models used to be thirty years old and glamorous.
Even if they were younger, with pancake makeup,
powder, rouge, false eyelashes, they looked thirty.
Then Swinging London invented youth and models
took off their makeup and looked their age. Twenty.*

Every little girl wanted to be a model. In the sixties, Blow-up, about a leading photographer (based on David Bailey) and his teen age models—who took their clothes off!—shocked the world. It glamourised drugs. In one scene, Verushka, at a London party was asked, "I thought you were in Paris?" "I am in Paris . . . " she replied.

Today, models are fifteen, even thirteen. Earning millions of dollars. The wasp-waisted fifties, the knock-kneed sixties, the slouchy seventies, the bag-lady early eighties and the *Dynasty* late eighties, the silicone-strut nineties and the grunge nineties each produced an ideal woman.

Fiona Campbell-Walter, Twiggy, Jean Shrimpton, any Annie Hall, street-cred models, Dalma, Patti Cleveland, Christie Turlington, Linda Evangelista, Cindy Crawford, Claudia Schiffer, Naomi Campbell, Kate Moss, Inès de la Fressange, Iman, Jerry Hall and Verushka (encore), Gisele Bündchen, Erin O'Connor, Alex Wek (the two easiest to draw) all had their day in the sun.

Black models, red-haired models, models who looked like boys (and boys who looked like girls) and many, many more were seen, in turn, on catwalks and pages of magazines.

The twenty-first century
has not yet produced
anything distinctive.
Today models
look, well,
interchangeable.

Body-type changes: A long torso and endless legs were symbols of the fifties and sixties; posture was a sign of the nineties; grunge was a slouch; silicone was—chest OUT!

Brit snobbery produced Honor Fraser,
from the Lovat Frasers,
Jasmine Guinness, brewing,
Stella Tennant,
the Duchess of Devonshire's granddaughter,
Jodie Kidd,
great-granddaughter of Lord Beaverbrook.

Dalma and Patti Cleveland (one of Antonio Lopez's girls) were the last models who knew how to walk. Patti could pirouette, dance, turn on a dime, all the while buttoning or unbuttoning a jacket.

Later, models seem to have received their training from the Spanish Riding School in Vienna. They stepped like Lippizaners. Claudia Schiffer walked like a farmhand.

It was Gianni Versace and Karl Lagerfeld who created the supermodel by paying her a fortune. Supermodels became stars. They always believed in their own press and never believed it when they found a wrinkle.

In the early nineties there were numerous memorable Model Moments when silicone-enhanced supermodels and bedraggled exponents of grunge confronted one another on fashion runways. My favourite moment came when Polly Mellen, still at Allure, announced, "Linda (Evangelista) is so hippy." Many, I'm sure, would like hips as big as Linda's.

Robert Altman created
an ultimate model moment
in *Prêt-à-Porter*
using real models
in a nude fashion show,
with a nude, pregnant bride,
Ute Lemper.

After the July 1993 CC HAUTE COUTURE at L'École des Beaux Arts, **Kate Moss** emerged with a BACCHUS hairstyle and SID VICIOUS **fuck-you** T-shirt.

She was **NOT** pleased. Karl had put her into only ONE show.

Franco Moschino (1950-1994).
In 1998 he turned in his GRAVE, winked and gave THE FINGER.

Naturally, San Francisco readers protested.

(San Franciso Examiner Magazine, October 1998)

GLAM'n GRUNGE, right. In 1993, KATE MOSS was 19 years old, 5'7" tall, 100 lbs, never worked out, SMOKED, DRANK, ate whatever she liked. CINDY CRAWFORD, 27, 5'9", 125 lbs, worked out, ate vegetables, never smoked, rarely drank (Self, July 1993)

time to change
into a 'New MODEL'
1

REMOVE SILICONE
LIPOSUCTION IMPLANTS
With PLASTIC surgery
2.

ADD TATTOO
OO!
remove EYEBROWS
4.

Major SURGERY
SHORTEN my legs

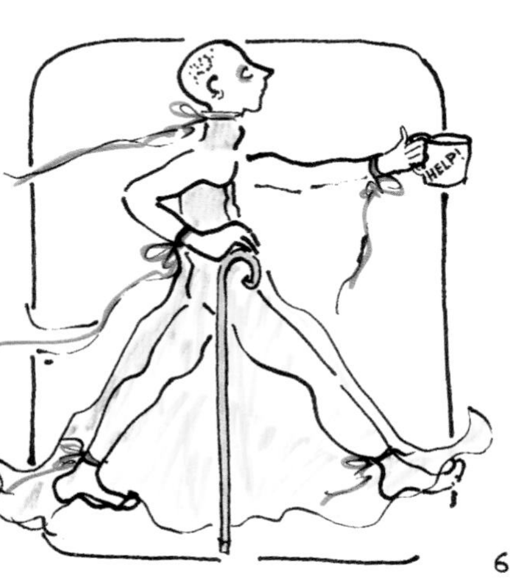

Cartoon from SILICONE to GRUNGE, from Supermodel to beggar, appeared in Mirabella, September 1993

Jean Paul Gaultier admitted to COLIN McDOWELL, "I have the taste of a concierge." In October 1996, Gaultier expressed his frustration with a funny and VULGAR collection. He was NOT PLEASED WITH THE PRESS. The only privately owned French fashion magazine, L'Officiel, was banned from his show. It was LATE IN THE EVENING, in the **red light district** of Paris, and everybody was tired by the time the BRIDE, **Easter lily up her BUM** MOONED the audience. The late **LIZ TILBERIS**, editor-in-chief of Harper's Bazaar, sitting **FRONT ROW CENTRE**, sighed, "I really did not need that."

"It seldom pays to
be rude; it never
pays to be only
half rude."
(Norman Douglas)

In March 1991, LINDA EVANGELISTA, just turned 30, wearing Chanel told the press to GET LOST, SWORE, then roared away on the back of a Harley Davidson.
(Elle UK, July, 1991)

LAETITIA SCHERRER with RABBIT

Was her father, JEAN-LOUIS SCHERRER's

Bride in 1991.

After M. Scherrer sold his name and lost his job, his daughter became a RABID ANIMAL ACTIVIST demonstrating outside fashion shows

(L'Officiel, June 1991)

Orange-haired Purple-dressed JERRY HALL ALWAYS A *favourite* on the RUNWAY modelled in VIVIENNE WESTWOOD'S Spring 1997 Collection.

(Punch, November, 1996)

LE MUSÉE DU MOYEN AGE THERMES DE CLUNY IS AN EXQUISITE MUSEUM/ ROMAN BATHS IN THE FIFTH ARRONDISSEMENT. THE DIRECTOR OF PRÊT-À-PORTER HAD BANNED PHOTOGRAPHERS FROM THE SET.
"HOW CAN WE HAVE A FASHION SHOW WITHOUT PHOTOGRAPHERS?" SOMEONE ASKED. THE ANSWER WAS SIMPLE.
"HOW CAN WE HAVE A FASHION SHOW WITHOUT CLOTHES?"
AT 7:45 P.M. ON WEDNESDAY APRIL 13, 1994, BACKSTAGE, THE MODELS WERE WEARING POINTY YELLOW MOROCCAN SLIPPERS AND TOWELLING COATS OR BODY SUITS.
THEY WERE **BUSY** APPLYING MAKEUP ON BRUISES AND BLEMISHES.
THE ICE WAS BROKEN WHEN THE PREGNANT BRIDE, **UTE LEMPER**, ANNOUNCED, "I NEVER MARRIED. I'M AGAINST MARRIAGE. I CAN'T MARRY AS LONG AS I DON'T HAVE A **CONTRACT**."

The July 1999 **DIOR** Haute Couture show took place in L'ORANGERIE at Versailles. The LONGEST runway was covered in water-filled plastic cushioning (like a giant WATER BED). There were models in jungle makeup and fan-shaped hair; and JOHN GALLIANO with his new distressed RED hair; and a gender-BENDER boy who opened the show and a MAGENTA and SCARLET finale **parachute** dress.

Break dancing at Michiko Koshino in LONDON.
(Punch, October, 1996)

PEDRO ALMODOVAR, Minnie Driver and a BENCHFUL of (anonymous) celebrities rate GISELE BÜNDCHEN at Versace, March 2000.

OOOOH!

OH!

ONLY ISSEY MIYAKE
T-SHIRTS-BY-THE

COULD HAVE COME UP WITH
MILE IN 1999........

SOPHIE DAHL is the granddaughter of Roald DAHL who wrote 'THE BFG' (Big Friendly Giant) for Young Sophie. She is much **SLIMMER** now. Roald also wrote 'Chitty Chitty Bang Bang' perhaps for an older SOPHIE, modelling in **JEAN PAUL Gaultier's** January 2001 HAUTE COUTURE Collection. (Sunday Times Style, February 4, 2001)

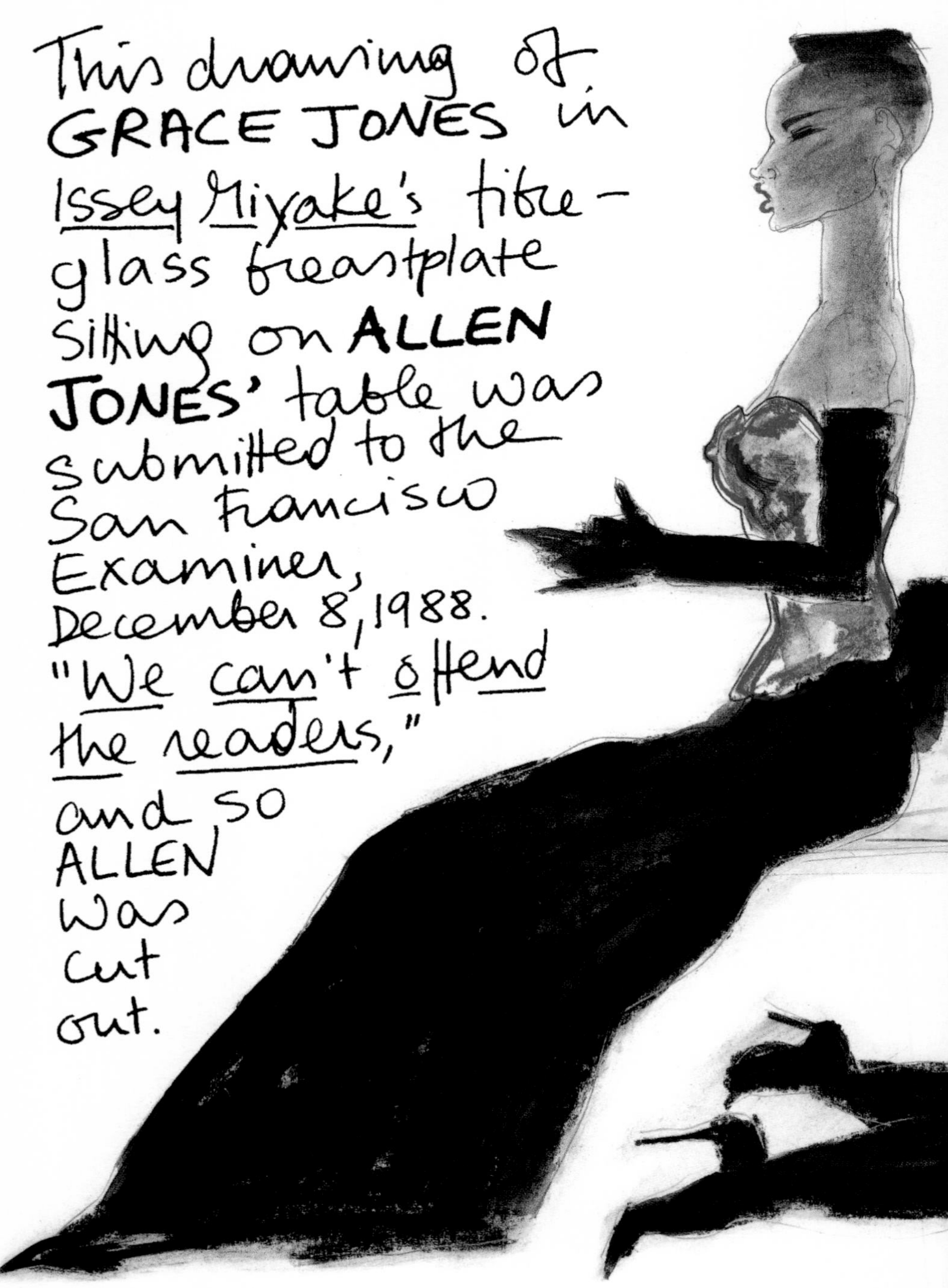
This drawing of
GRACE JONES in
Issey Miyake's fibre-
glass breastplate
sitting on ALLEN
JONES' table was
submitted to the
San Francisco
Examiner,
December 8, 1988.
"We can't offend
the readers,"
and so
ALLEN
was
cut
out.

In May 1991, **Metropolis** printed the whole drawing. CLEARLY, <u>their</u> readers are <u>harder</u> <u>to</u> <u>offend</u>.

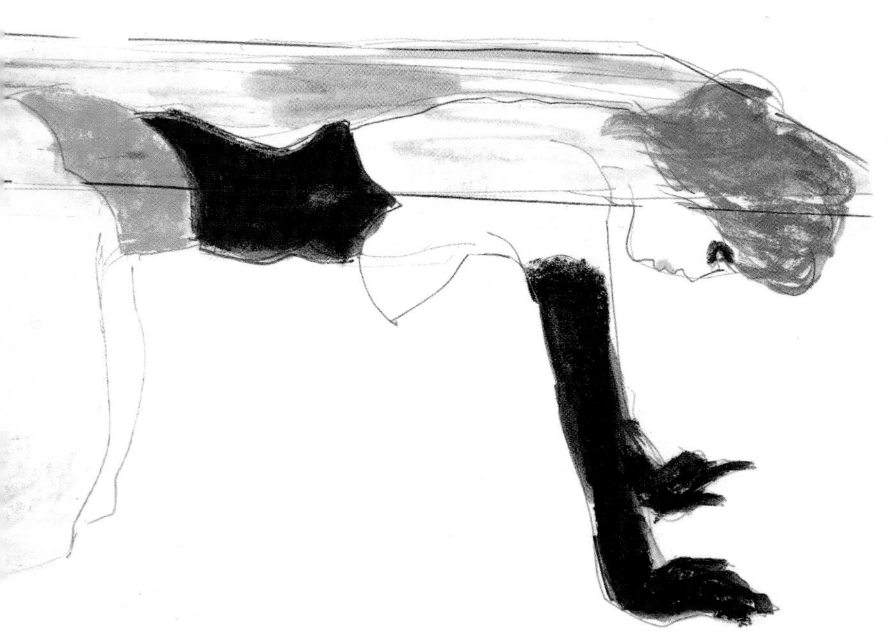

1990 was the
YEAR of the
Big Pink Hair
with
Rifat
Ozbek's
red dress.
(Joyce Magazine,
Holiday, 1990)

In Autumn 1994, **NADIA AUERMANN**'s agent specified WHICH MODEL should precede and follow her on the runway. I paired her with **KATE MOSS**, surely a NO-NO.

The HOTTEST fashion show in PARIS, including a fur skirt, took place on July 18, 1999 when JEAN PAUL GAULTIER showed his Haute Couture Collection at the Hôtel de Poulpry, built in 1697 by la Baronne de Poulpry. (Talk, October 1999)

WHAT'S BLACK AND WHITE AND RED ALL OVER?

Naomi Campbell in VERSACE'S March 1994 Collection. (Drawn for the B.B.C.)

WHAT'S BLACK AND WHITE DOGSTOOTH BLOWING RED KISSES ALL OVER?

Jean Paul Gaultier's MYSTERY model, October 1991.

AZZEDINE ALAÏA is generous to his friends. In October 1991, he lent LA VERRERIE to Vivienne WESTWOOD, Designer of the Year, who unveiled a collection accessorised with SEX TOYS.

(Yup, that's a GOLDEN DILDO...)

(Elle, U.K February 1992)

This drawing, from **PACO RABANNE's** January 1998 Haute Couture was <u>FIRMLY</u>

<u>REJECTED</u> by the Sunday Times Style.

("*We* are a *family* magazine.")

"FASHION IS GENTILITY
RUNNING AWAY FROM
VULGARITY AND AFRAID
OF BEING OVERTAKEN."
(Hazlitt).
I loved drawing
this Thierry MUGLER
dress from his March
1995 collection.
To wear?
I prefer to
COVER
MY
BACK-
SIDE.
(ELLE, August 1995)

Jean Paul Gaultier's BALD model with stars on tits — MADONNA Style — paraded in the March 1992 show. (GRAZIA April 10, 1992; The Sunday Times Style, family magazine, also ran this drawing, September 17, 2000.)

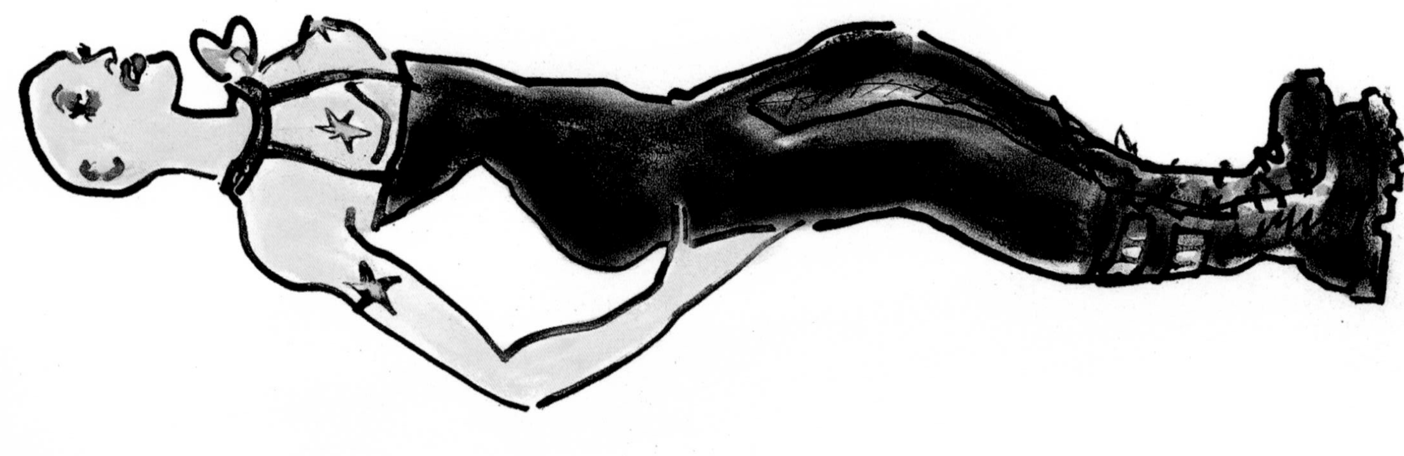

Model **Erin O'Connor** is Une JOLIE-LAIDE and very easy to draw. In January 1998, Karl Lagerfeld got her in the SACK. A Haute Couture sack, naturally.

Another exquisite Jean Paul Gaultier collection – tattoos, piercings, some real, some faux. (Los Angeles Times, November 1993.)

Paco Rabanne takes shelter under his bride after his Haute Couture Collection in July 1997.

The MARCH 1994 **GAULTIER** show with **ROSSY de PALMA** and an **ESKIMO** took place in a freezing depôt, with artificial snow on the floor that made us COUGH AND CRY.

A FAKE ICE RINK at the CIRQUE d'HIVER was the setting for GAULTIER's MARCH 1991 Collection. NOBODY GOT SICK. (Grazia, November 1991)

Model GEORGIANNA ROBERTSON played a model in Robert Altman's 1995 film Prêt-à-Porter. Before the film, her career was flourishing. After the film, she had a hard time getting jobs in PARIS. She cropped her hair and BLEACHED it BLONDE. YVES SAINT LAURENT ALWAYS USED HER.

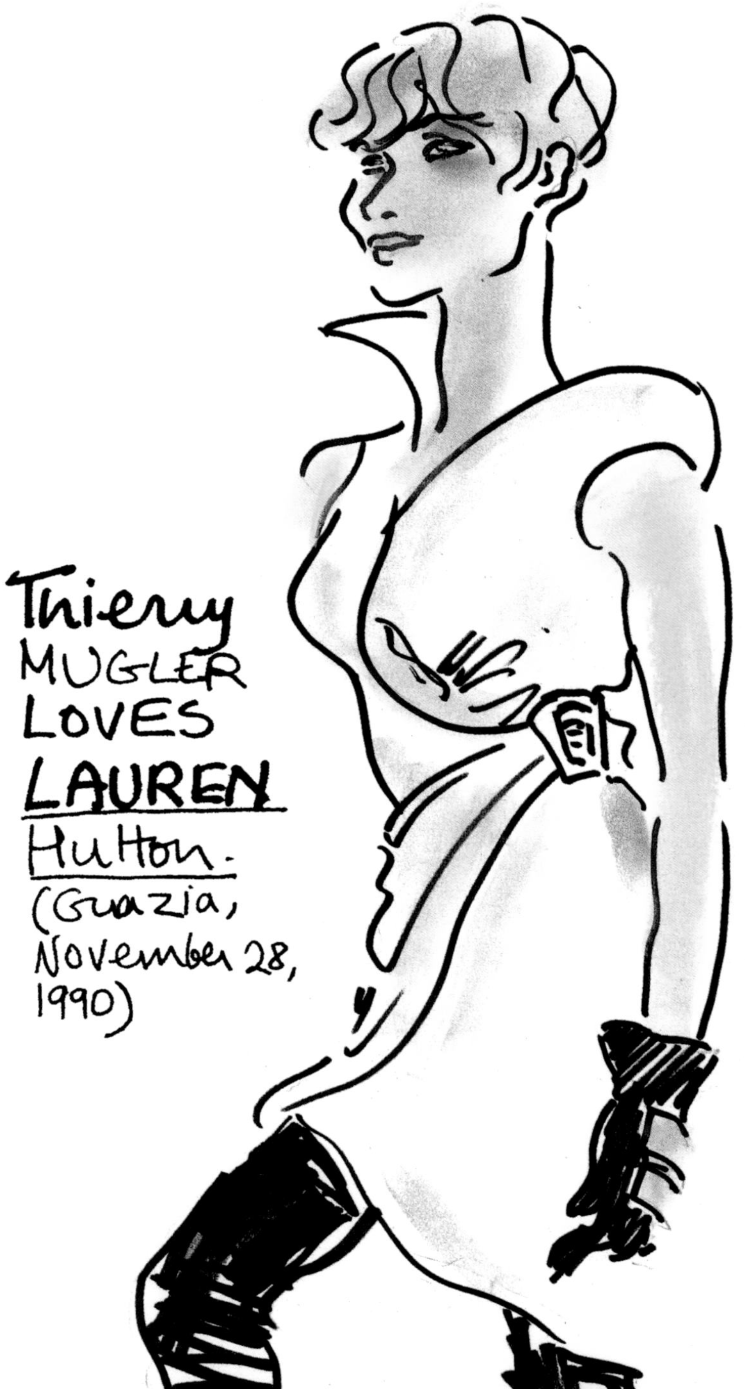
Thierry
MUGLER
LOVES
LAUREN
Hutton.
(Grazia,
November 28,
1990)

OPPOSITE: McQueen's <u>tortures</u> promote VOWS OF **SILENCE** and **FASTING**. (TRENDSETTER COVER, MAY 2001)

ALEX WEK gets <u>gilded</u> for the JULY 2001 **DIOR** Haute Couture

LEFT, RIGHT
LEFT, RIGHT

AFTER the DIOR Collection in March 2000, Gisele Bündchen is disabled BY TWO manicurists.

VIVIENNE WESTWOOD'S BOTTOM LINE WOULD HAVE PLEASED THE LATE JAMES LAVER WHOSE THEORY OF THE SHIFTING EROGENOUS ZONE CAUSED A RIOT IN 1969. (L'Officiel, May, 1994)

6
PRESS & PHOTOGRAPHERS

There is the glossy
magazine press;
the newspaper press;
the American press;
the foreign press;
the television press
and the unimportant press.
They all chew gum.

Editors of glossies absolutely must dress the part because for about an hour before every collection, they are inspected and criticized. What they wear, who they wear, how they sit, how they laugh, who they talk to, are scrutinised and picked over. When gossip and speculation swirls about their job (Kate Betts, ex-American Harper's Bazaar, Joan Buck, ex-French Vogue, Carine Roitfeld, French Vogue) they must look serene and answer rude questions.

Grace Coddington of American Vogue told me, "There's what I say, there's what I think and there's what I really think." Glossies go to grand dinners every night to please the advertisers. They must suppress irony. Better yet, they should possess none. Irony is for the newspaper fashion critics, though few exercise this right, fearing they may lose out on freebies, dinners and front row seats.

Newspaper reporters,
especially New Yorkers,
talk non-stop throughout fashion shows.
They eat, slurp and often look
totally unfashionable.
However if they write well
—and a few do—
they are forgiven.

Over the years, I have worked for American, British, French, Italian and Japanese publications. There is a national consensus. For example, when the Americans loved a Dolce & Gabbana collection, the British and French loathed it. The seventies-inspired thrift-shop collection entitled 'Banal,' by Miuccia Prada, made the Italians furious and thrilled the British.

Seating is sacred.
No journalist would relinquish his seat.
The ninety-plus-year-old
Eleanor Lambert
was told by an inexperienced publicist
with a historic name
that she must stand in the back.
Fortunately, Ms. Lambert
was recognized by a senior executive
and swiftly seated.

There was one exception when the dashing Gilles Bensimon of American ELLE, *with a charming habit of kissing women's hands, offered his seat to the late Liz Tilberis of American* Harper's Bazaar. *Jaws hit chests.*

fashion photographers have a terrible time, jammed into tiny spaces, waiting hours for a show to begin. Woe betide anyone with an upset stomach. Every now and then, photographers revolt. They start a fight. They sing the "Marseillaise." They sing "Happy Birthday." They walk out. Then they creep back. The fact is, they cannot afford to boycott a collection. There is always a house photographer to distribute pictures. Sometimes the scene turns ugly. A large Korean photographer, banned from London, turns up regularly in Paris. He uses his metal box and tripod as battering rams. In his wake, Manolo-shod editors are left nursing bleeding ankles and shins.

Injuries occur.
Reactions differ.
At Matthew Williamson's
February 2001
show in London,
a large speaker
fell off the wall hitting
a *L'Officiel* editor.
The show was interrupted
while blood,
spurting from a head wound,
was mopped
and the ambulance arrived.
Then the show continued.
"Poor Matthew,"
remarked
Helena Christiensen.
"His show was messed up."
Such bad luck.

TWO GUYS, MAUD MOLYNEUX, left, in YSL and Michel CRESSOLE on the terrace of the CERCLE DE L'UNION INTERALLIÉE for the

Chambre Syndicale's SUMMER party. (L'Officiel, June ; 1991)

I put PEN to PAPER
et Voilà! Kim Hastreiter...

VISION
AIR

DO THEY SHARE A VISION? Cecilia Dean, far left, and HARPER'S BAZAAR'S STEPHEN GAN and GLENDA BAILEY

HARPER'S BAZAAR

ADVERTISERS

At Condé Nast you need a NOSE for FASHION:

Hamish Bowles (American Vogue) left; LINDA Wells (ALLURE); Gene KRELL (Japanese, Korean, Taiwan Vogues).

BODY LANGUAGE BEFORE Givenchy, July, 1999.
BERNARD ARNAULT and Jamie SAMET have a tête-à-tête or maybe a stomach-à-stomach.

LET ANY MINION DARE TO STOP THEM. **GILLES Bensimon** of American ELLE and **ANGELICA Blechschmidt** of German VOGUE, take runway photos even if it is STRICTLY INTERDIT and **absolutely DÉFENDU**.

Barbara WALTERS gets MIKED after Calvin Klein's October 1992 COLLECTION

CARINE ROITFELD, editor-in-chief of French Vogue, former Gucci stylist, KAL RUTTENSTEIN'S muse, at the MARCH 2002 collections, in shoes by CESARE PIACIOTTI

In September 1992, **LIZ TILBERIS** launched her first Harper's Bazaar. On August 30, 1992, the **NEW YORK TIMES** Magazine ran this drawing with the caption, THE NEW EDITOR-IN-CHIEF OF HARPER'S BAZAAR KNOWS WHAT SHE WANTS: NUMBER 93 IN THE CALVIN KLEIN SHOW.

With little else to occupy us at the February 2002 FASHION WEEK in London, we relished the duel between COLIN McDOWELL, ace fashion writer and NICHOLAS COLERIDGE, Chairman of the BRITISH FASHION COUNCIL and Managing Director of CONDÉ NAST BRITAIN.

SO GOOD FOR THEM TO WALK TWENTY PACES AT DAWN

RIGHT! HELPS THE CIRCULATION!

SUNDAY TIMES STYLE

EVENING STANDARD

SECOND(S) TO NONE

Since then, SUNDAY TIMES and Robert Johnston have parted and Jeremy Langmead left the Evening Standard to edit WALLPAPER

The French fashion press in Paris is aloof. THEY RARELY MIX WITH FOREIGNERS. They are SUPERIOR. They speak the LANGUAGE. Yet, there is RESENTMENT towards **Americans** who get the . . .

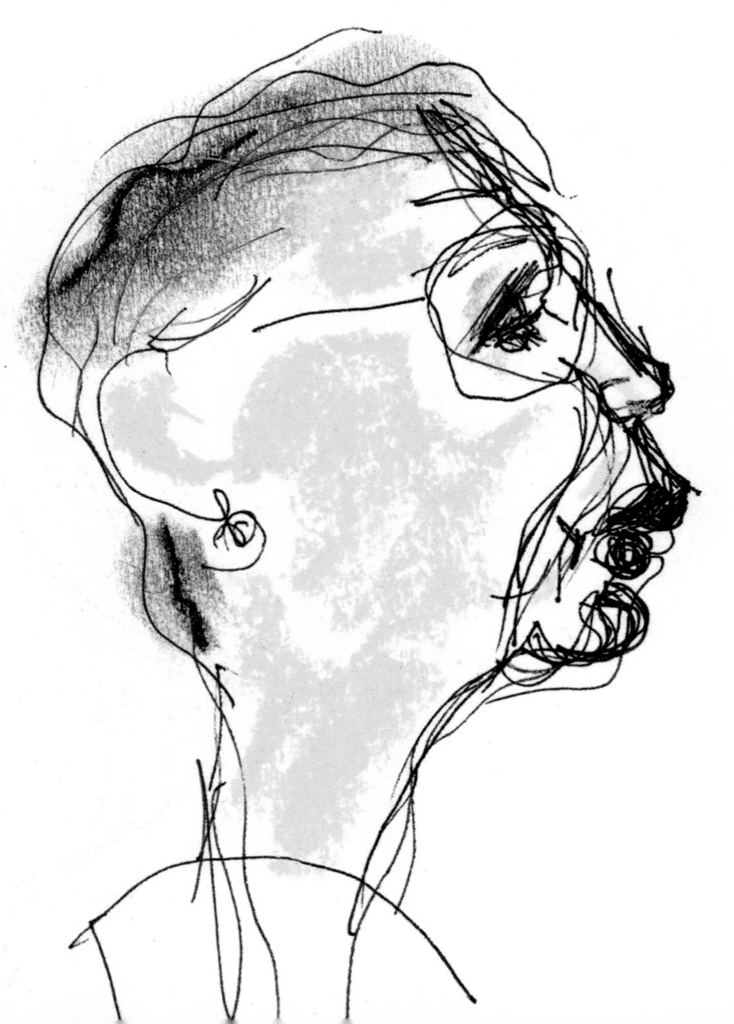

... **BIGGEST and BEST** seat allocations at the shows. THESE TRICOTEUSES WATCH AND WAIT. On this page, JACKIE Malissen, ex Marie Claire. Opposite, the free-lancer **Melka** TREATON.

OPPOSITE: ETTA FROIO OF WOMEN'S WEAR DAILY. LIKE the MONA LISA, there is always a small smile hovering... if butter doesn't melt in Etta's MOUTH, WHO DISPATCHES THOSE BARBED WIRES?

THIS PAGE: NATALIA ASPESI of La Repubblica. THE COSY Ms. ASPESI looks as though she stepped out of BEATRIX POTTER, but she HARBOURS FANTASIES OF wearing a SEXY MUGLER suit.

French and FrANGLAIS

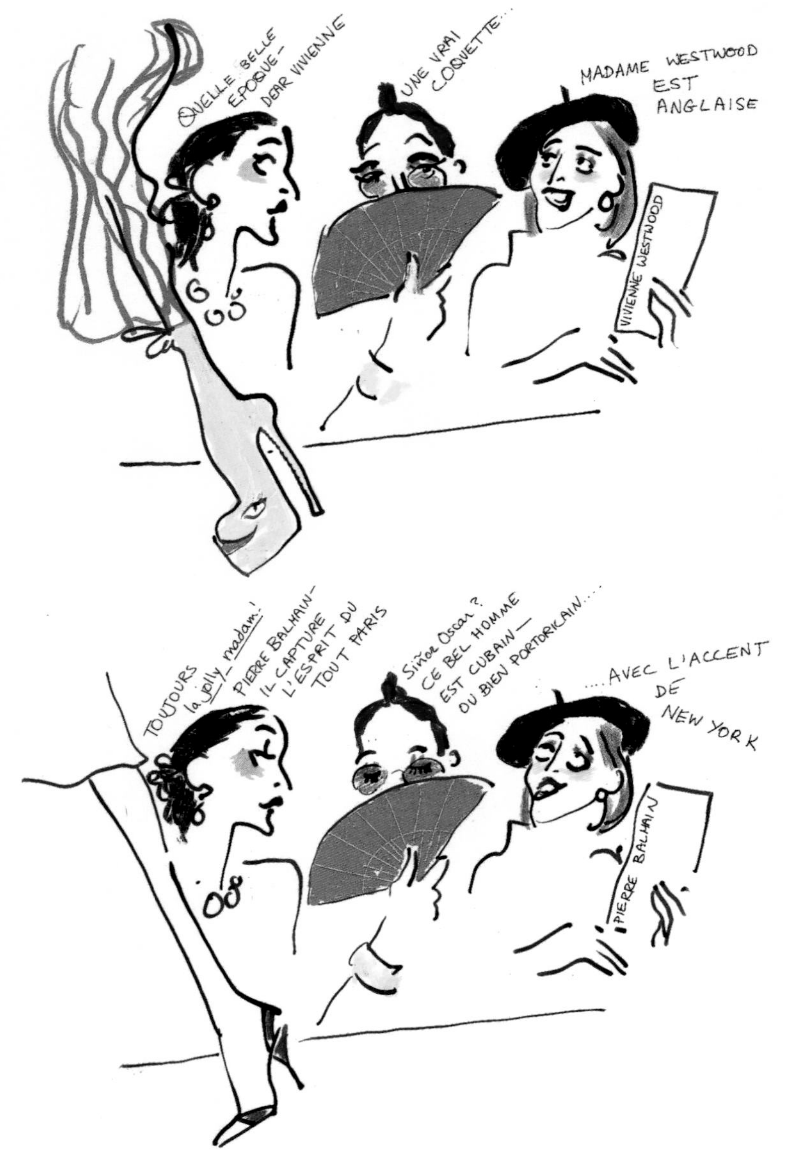

PARIS IS THE CAPITAL OF FASHION....

But how many FRENCH DESIGNERS clog the catwalks? (L'Officiel, October 1992).

LA SIMPLICITE DE GIVENCHY. ON NE PEUT GALLIC!
C'EST WONDERFUL!
MONSIEUR GALLIANO EST UN SUJET BRITANNIQUE....
EN PASSANT PAR GIBRALTAR
GIVENCHY
ANN DEMEULEMEESTER, C'EST TOUT LE FRENCH EXISTENTIALISM!
TOUT A FAIT ÇA!
C'EST AUSSI UNE PLAISANTERIE BELGE....
DEMEULEMEESTER

OH! CHANEL EST SO ROMANCE
BIEN DE CHEZ NOUS, N'EST-CE PAS?
NON. HERR LAGERFELD EST ALLEMAND.
AH! L'ELEGANCE DE CHRISTIAN DIOR! VERY CHIC!
TRES PARISIAN!
SIGNOR FERRÉ EST ITALIEN....
CHRISTIAN DIOR

Photographer
STEVEN MEISEL
(with hat) and
Mademoiselle
BENJAMIN
get Front
Row seats.

FABIEN BARON
designed the CK logo,
Issey Miyake's perfume
bottle and MADONNA'S
book. Some say that
Fabien, a friend of Calvin
Klein, invented KATE
MOSS. The rest of the RUMOURS
about him are
UNPRINTABLE
(L'Officiel, November, 1994.)

Faces in my sketchbook: INGRID SISCHY of Interview, right, and POLLY Mellen, then at ALLURE.

LAUREN EZERSKY, the impossibly CHIC writer for PAPER, wore a Gaultier skirt to Dries Van NOTEN's collection.

(JOYCE MAGAZINE AUTUMN 1994.)

SUPER LENSWOMAN **Annie LEIBOVITZ** and MASTER CLIQUER Mario TESTINO never said CHEESE. Maybe NEVER MET?

ese, Mario!
maggio, Annie!

CLICK CLIQUE CLAQUE: ROXANNE Lowitt explains runway to **RICHARD Avedon** at the MUSÉE RODIN IN 2001. (These two *did* meet).

first you focus...
...then you shoot

HELMUT NEWTON, WHO ELSE, IN PRÊT-À-PORTER AT LEDOYEN ON MARCH 10, 1994. HELMUT, TAKING PICTURES, WAS FOLLOWED BY **PARIS PREMIÈRE** VIDEO TEAM, WHO FILMED HIM PHOTOGRAPHING, AND BY 2 ASSISTANTS, ONE TECHNICAL, ONE HUMAN, TAKING COPIOUS NOTES. WHEN ASKED, WHY THE ENTOURAGE? "BECAUSE I'M SO IMPORTANT." HE SNAPPED WITHOUT BLOODY IRONY.

ALEXANDRA Shulman arrived at BRITISH VOGUE (here at the October 1992 Collections) in a burgundy velvet dress with a draped top.

BY OCTOBER 1996 BRITISH VOGUE had ARRIVED AT ALEX SHULMAN IN A BLUE DRESS WITH draped top.

After
CNN cancelled
STYLE WITH ELSA KLENSCH,
in February 2001 there
was NOTHING to watch at
7:30 a.m. (PACIFIC TIME).

HAZARDS OF THE FRONT ROW: CROSS

YOUR LEGS, EDITORS, AND WAKE UP!
MARCH 2000.

RAPT IN RAP at TOMMY Hilfiger's 1996 collection in LONDON: Hilary Alexander, fashion editor of the Telegraph, was transported by TREACH, lead singer

of Naughty BY NATURE, as his PANTS SLOWLY DESCENDED...

POLLY MELLEN HAS MANY SIDES. Drawn in 2001.

7 TRENDSETTERS

Catherine de Medici, not Galliano, invented the fishtail.
She also invented high heels. Not Manolo.
Chanel invented the little black dress and branding.
Madeleine Vionnet invented the bias cut.
Madonna reinvents herself constantly.
Now she is the huntin', shootin', fish wife.
A trendsetter is opinionated and mysterious.
Diana Vreeland's origins
and age changed with each telling.
Vivienne Westwood is a mad trendsetter
and has remained poor.
Yves Saint Laurent is a classic trendsetter and grew rich.

Buñuel's 1967 film Belle du Jour was re-released in the cinemas in 1995. It starred Catherine Deneuve dressed by Yves Saint Laurent—at his best. In 1996, Prada introduced a Belle du Jour Collection. The princess coat with the half belt at the back, the box pleats, the squared-off pump. It was a big hit. A season or two later, the house of Genny knocked off Prada. Sitting in the front row at the Genny show in Milan was Catherine Deneuve.

For some trendsetters
dressing (up) is a creative process.
They are true eccentrics
who express themselves by,
or hide behind, costume.
Examples: Zandra Rhodes,
Anna Piaggi, Isabella Blow.

Dress is an indicator of class. In the Bible Belt, for example, women celebrate Christmas with an explosion of red and green lurex sweaters ablaze with Santa, elves and Rudolf. Flight attendants wear red and green glass Christmas tree decorations around their necks and dangling from their ears. Some southern belle must have started this. It did not start in Paris.

Style is a code that changes like slang. Whether it is outrageous haute couture worn by nouveau riche or grunge from Seattle or Christmas sweaters or the little black dress or a torn, patched tweed hacking jacket worn by the Duke of Norfolk, it makes a statement about the wearer. It shows (on the part of the duke) total self confidence and disdain.

The church has influence.
Mario Boselli, president of Italian fashion,
owns a textile factory
that used to be a church.
The Venice pad of Beppe Modenese,
the honorary president,
was also once a church.

A trend happens. Patrick Cabasset of L'Officiel explained, "Everyone agrees. There is red. There is white. There is blue. Then someone comes along and says, 'It is not blue anymore.'" Audrey Hepburn made bosoms passé. Princess Diana made long hair passé. Carine Roitfeld makes good health positively unwholesome.

A trendsetter knows when to wear a ton of pearls.
When to wear distressed denim.
When to wear a huge hat.
When to take off the hat.
When to stop wearing old Burberry and Prada.
When to eat fast food.
When to eat slow food.
When to straighten and thin out your hair (Now!).
When to get very thin (Right now!).

"Everyone was intrigued by
the Duchess of Windsor,"
recalled Givenchy.
"Everyone wanted to know
what she was buying."
On one occasion,
eight women turned up
to a party wearing copies
of a horizontally striped dress
Givenchy made for the duchess.
She laughed it off
and started a conga line.

THE CONTENTS OF AN ENTIRE (PALOMA PICASSO) LIPSTICK WAS USED ON THE BACKGROUND....

NEW YORK <u>fashionistas</u> never take a <u>BUS</u>. Unless it is A <u>JITNEY</u>.

GAP

THE ITALIAN POLICE HAVE NAPOLEONIC CHIC.

FRENCH POLICE ROLLERBLADE AFTER FASHION VICTIMS....

"AS A GENERAL RULE, NOBODY HAS
MONEY WHO OUGHT TO HAVE IT."
(DISRAELI). DENISE HALE
IS THE ONLY SAN
FRANCISCAN IN THE WORLD
IN THE BEST DRESSED
HALL OF FAME. FOR
THE OPENING OF THE OPERA
IN 1988 SHE WORE
A $27,000 GIANFRANCO
FERRÉ CREATION,
"HEAVILY DISCOUNTED."
HER ESCORT
WAS FERRÉ.

TOM FORD finds the prettiest BOYS IN PARIS TO FORM an honour guard at the MUSEE RODIN leading into the Yves Saint Laurent Collection.

a little fancy footwork
at Byron Lars

a little elevation at
Gaultier....

a little HELP

a little
soap box
UP
to...

This Political PLATFORM CARTOON was inspired by GIANTS, COSTUMES IN DAS RHEINGOLD and Raymond MASSARO's shoes, Spring 1992. (Montreal Gazette, September 15, 1992)

RECYCLED BURB FROM LONDON
NOWBURB
FREEBIE
PRADA
GIRLIE GALLIANO
WOOF!
BURP

FAUX BURB
PAS PRADA
STATUS BURB
CHECK:
FRINGE!
FOR
FALL
galliano
BURBERRY
fever and
Prada mania
swept THE
MARCH 2000
shows.
Naturally,
JOHN GALLIANO
took the Mick.

A BRITISH MOMENT AT Complice
(DESIGNED BY DOLCE E GABBANA)
IN OCTOBER
1992
(Madame,
January
1992)

AN AMERICAN
MOMENT
in New York
after
SEPTEMBER 11:
LIBERTY
FRATERNITY
and
FASHION!

"NOTHING IS ENOUGH FOR A MAN FOR WHOM ENOUGH IS TOO LITTLE." (EPICURUS). IN JANUARY 1991, DURING THE **GULF WAR**, ARAB **PRINCESSES**, STUCK AT HOME, WERE CLAMOURING FOR VIDEOS – ESPECIALLY

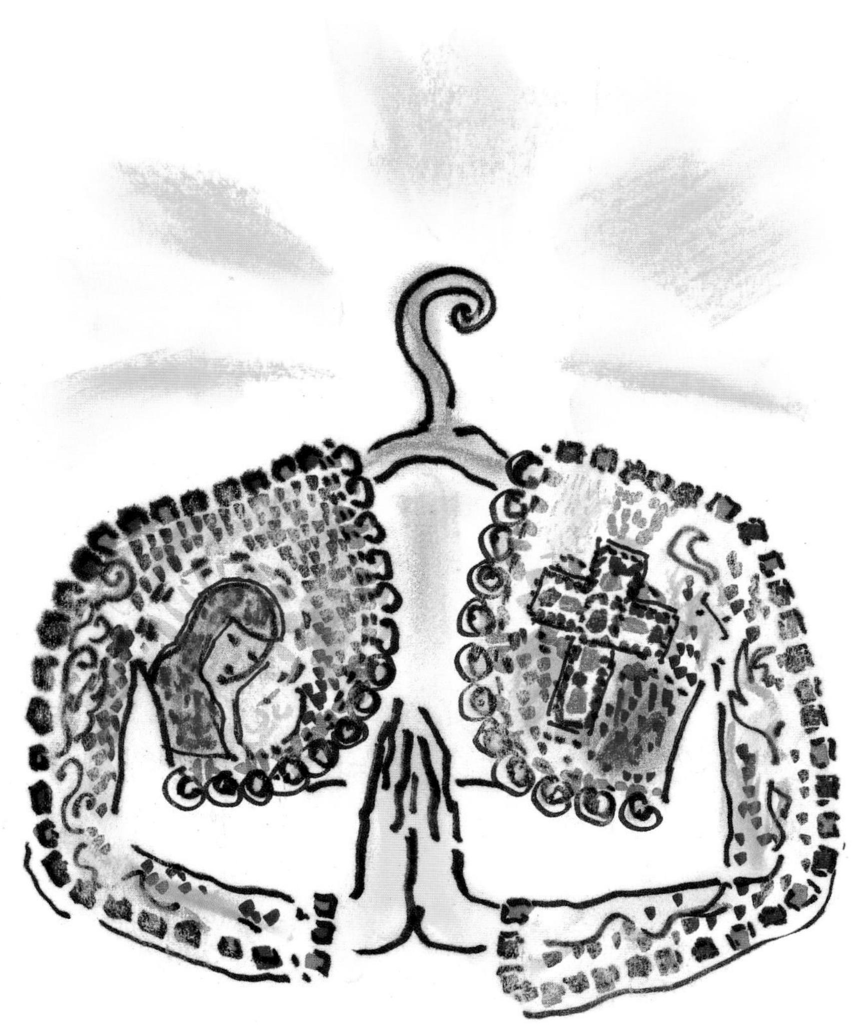

THOSE OF THE LOUIS FERAUD AND JEAN-LOUIS SCHERRER COLLECTIONS. THEY'D HAVE LOVED THESE **MADONNA** (VIRGIN NOT SINGER) JACKETS BY VERSACE. (MIRABELLA, MAY, 1991)

ROSSY de PALMA, Anouk Aimée's assistant in Prêt-a-Porter, wearing YVES SAINT LAURENT HAUTE COUTURE, March 10, 1994

WHAT A BORE. Poor STEPHEN JONES, he got much flack from the POLITICALLY CORRECT and humourless British press after the DIOR HAUTE COUTURE IN JULY 1999. "IF THIS HAD BEEN A REAL BOAR'S HEAD, IT WOULD HAVE BEEN TWICE AS BIG," HE SAID. (SAN FRANCISCO EXAMINER MAGAZINE, NOVEMBER 21, 1999)

LES MUSTS:
cigarette, lollipop,
chewing gum – <u>all</u> <u>together</u>.
MARCH 2000

LE LITTLE DOG: the DE RIGUEUR MINI Yorkie

FASHION? ART? IMPRESSIONISM?

Spring 1991
Ready-to-wear
coincided
with a
GIANT
Art fair
in paris

WE COMPARED
JOHN
GALLIANO
WITH
CÉSAR
Baldacchini

ANNA PIAGGI's hat by Stephen Jones mirrors Jean-Charles de CASTELBAJAC's HAUTE COUTURE MILLINARY in July 2000.

ALL LIT UP. Candles on Jean Paul Gaultier, left, Issey Miyake, right and police car light on Vivienne Westwood at the Paris ready-to-wear in March 1994 (Joyce Magazine, Autumn 1994)

In a story, VIVIENNE WESTWOOD DRESSES CELEBRITIES, I parked the police light on AZZEDIN ALAÏA, a good friend of Vivienne Westwood (L'Officiel, August 1994)

BRAVO! Rose
Marie rules
Britannia: in 1993
shortly before
his death,
FRANCO MOSCHINO
STAGED A TONGUE-IN-CHEEK
exhibition in MILAN. He dressed the
Queen of ENGLAND from head to
toe in BURBERRY. Little did he know
that by 2002, the American, ROSE
MARIE BRAVO (appointed CEO in 1997)

Would elevate the plaid to the THRONE

BUT ARE THEY WEARING UNDERWEAR? Alexander McQueen at the VH1/VOGUE AWARDS and Vivienne Westwood at YSL's farewell in January 2002

In SEPTEMBER 2000
BOY GEORGE d.j-ed
and

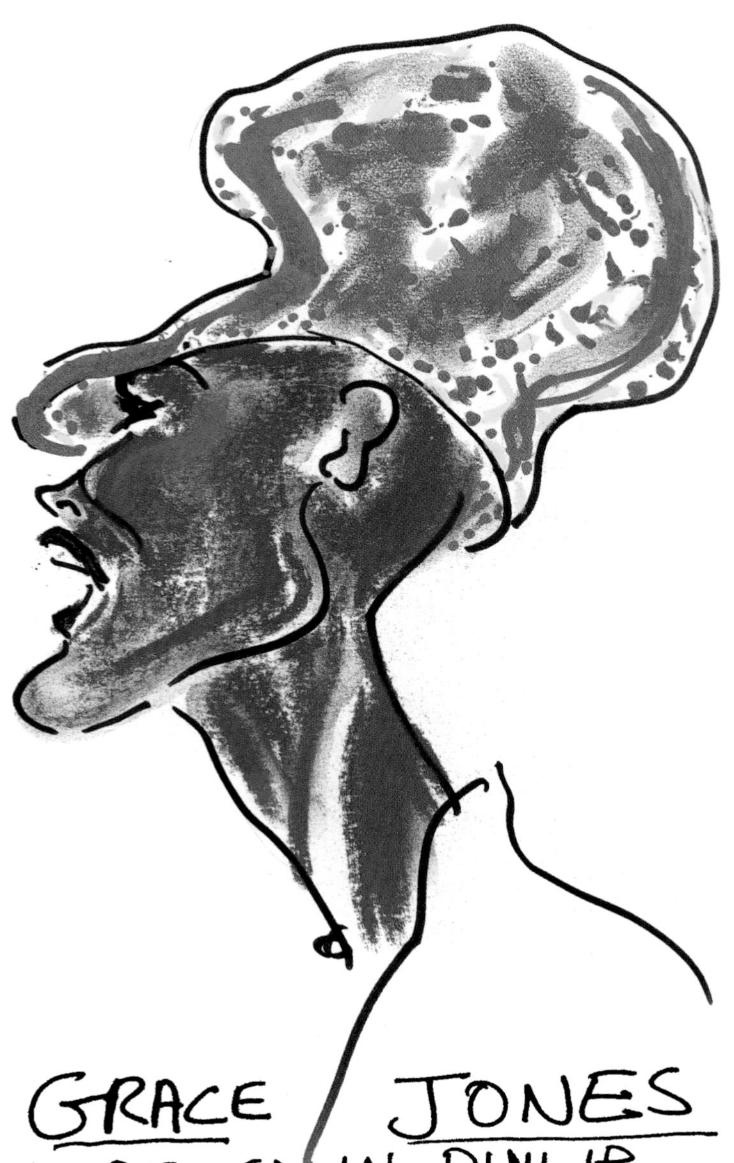

GRACE JONES
MODELLED IN PHILIP TREACY's Show at TIFFANY's in Bond Street

NEW YORK BAG LADY

PARIS BAG LADY

IL FAUT SOUFFRIR POUR ÊTRE BELLE. Or you can shoot from the hip. Or try LIPOSUCTION.
(Mirabella, July, 1992)
FEMME FATALE
FAT CAT

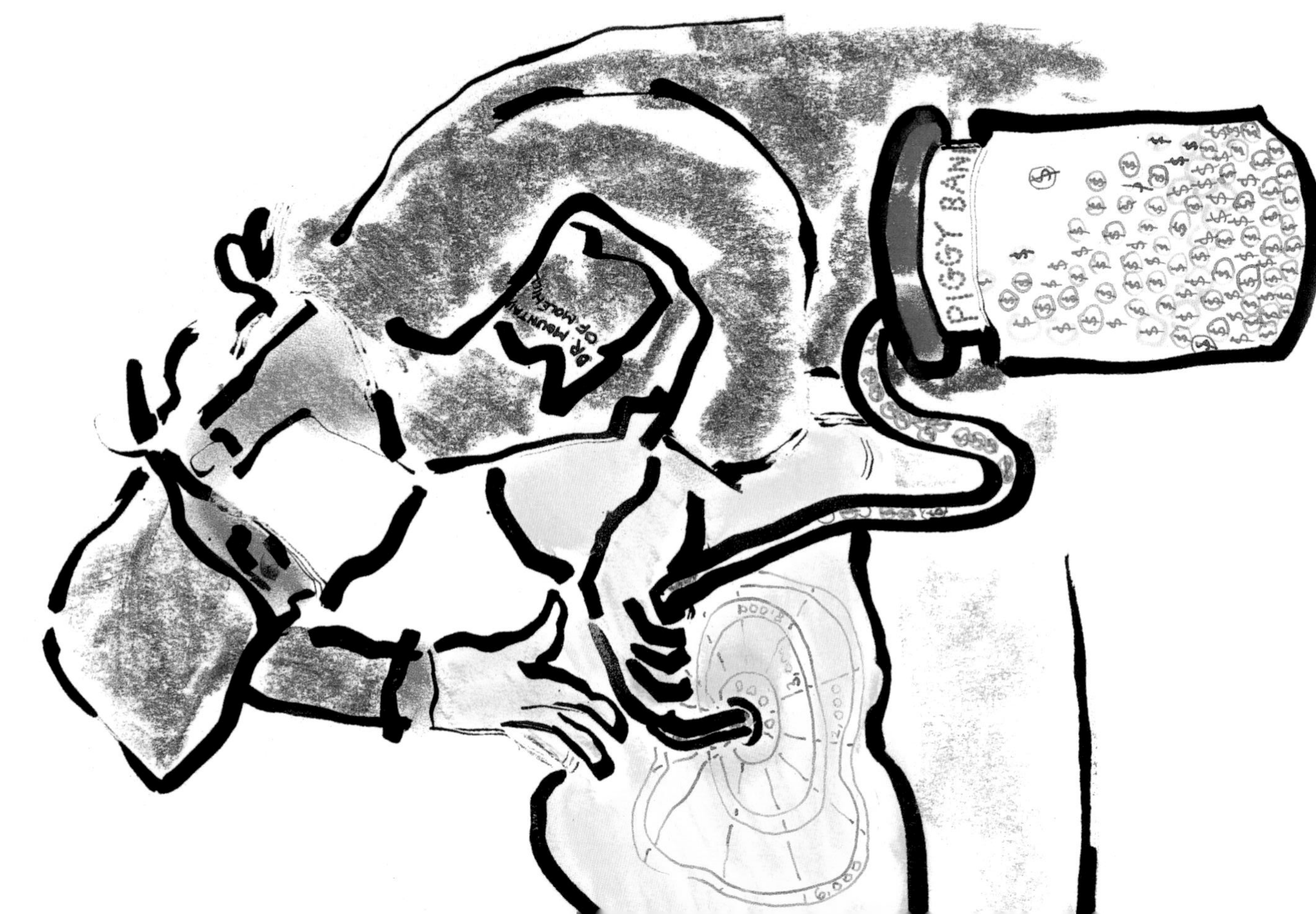
PIGGY BAN

JOHN GALLIANO (1995, 1994 and 1993) said: "THERE IS A whole generation of women who HAVE NOT EXPERIENCED the fit of a properly constucted jacket unless they happened to have CHANCED UPON a COUTURE JACKET in a

1995

FLEA MARKET (L'Officiel, August 1995)

BEND THE GENDER:
Jean Paul Gaultier's
male models prance
like WOMEN; some
FEMALE models
may be men;

THIS PLEASES THE FASHION PRESS because there is *plenty* of **cross-dressing** OFF THE CATWALK.

(Drawn for Fashion Television, July 1997)

IN LEAN
times
$ave
$ave
$ave
DRESS ON THE HOUSE

IN A BANDAGE

A BLANKET

CURTAINS! LIGHTBUL

"I DON'T MIND LYING, BUT I HATE INACCURACY." (Samuel Butler).

IN A DUVET

Every one of these garments paraded on the catwalks during the MARCH 1992 ready-to-wear collections. **IT IS CHEAPER TO DRESS ON THE HOUSE.** (Montreal Gazette, September 15, 1992)

OR
JUST A LAMPSHADE
(CHEAPER THAN GIGLI)

"NO ANIMAL ADMIRES ANOTHER ANIMAL." (Pascal).
This page: Philip Treacy's ANT EATER. (Australian Vogue March 1994.)

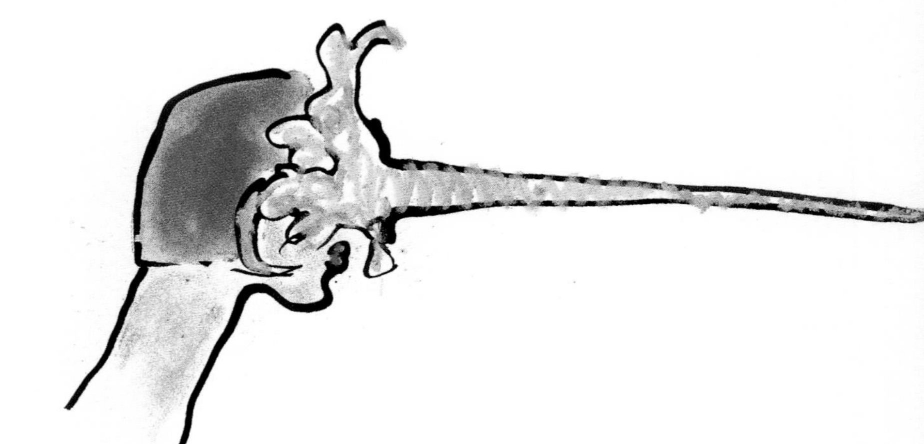

RENÉ GAULTIER, *right*, from SAINT-ASTIER in the DORDOGNE, uncle of **JEAN PAUL**, sported an elephant tusk protruding from his chest in July 1999. His wife, **LOUISETTE** Gaultier, was MUCH AMUSED....

ÉLÉPHANT!
GENTILHOMME?
BOURGEOIS ?

In the 18, JEAN PAUL GAULTIER would have quali-fied as one of

LES INCROYABLES

(L'Officiel, February, 1990)

Montserrat Caballé's dress form at the San Francisco Opera Costume Shop is INCREDIBLE

"LIFE IS NOT A SPECTACLE OR A FEAST; IT IS A PREDICAMENT." (SANTAYANA). THEIR ROYAL HIGHNESSES Prince Pavlos and Princess MARIE-Chantal of GREECE, in the FRONT ROW at Valentino's January 1999 HAUTE COUTURE, were hassled by M.C. SOLAR and Ophelie Winter holding the SAME SEAT NUMBERS. VENDEUSES WERE **hysterical**. ROYALISTS WERE **outraged**. REPUBLICANS WERE **unimpressed**. POP FANS were FURIOUS....

M.C.SOLAR!
Ophélie Winter!
Ophélie pas de place
those Greek PRETENDERS!
CATASTROPHE
BUM RAP
It's all GREEK to me.....

"LIFE IS TOO SHORT TO BE SMALL." (DISRAELI). The most elegant man in ITALY, **BEPPE** Modenese, of the Camera Nazionale della Moda Italiana, COULD TAKE A **HAT TIP** from HAMID **Karzai**, INTERIM PRESIDENT OF AFGHANISTAN, voted by **TOM** FORD, "the chicest man in the world" (ON OCTOBER 16, 2001). WEAR A JAUNTY CAP!

BRITISH FASHION EDITOR OF THE TELEGRAPH, HILARY ALEXANDER WORE AN I LOVE NEW YORK T SHIRT AND A UNION JACK...
CARDIGAN AFTER SEPTEMBER 11, 2001
I NY

FASHION
FAIRY TALES

THIS WAS PUBLISHED BY JOYCE MAGAZINE IN HONG KONG. AUTUMN 1993.

Once upon a time in the MAGIC Kingdom of COUTURE, there lived a little orphan called PRINCESS KATE. Kate had two wicked stepsisters, the PRINCESS LINDA and the PRINCESS CLAUDIA. Linda and Claudia were big and brash and Kate was small and sad...

In the castle next door lived two super-sniffers, the LADY CHRISTY and the LADY NAOMI, who went around all day with their noses in the air, waving a hanky

GLADYS PERINT PALMER IS SPELLBOUND BY THE AUTUMN Collections

Just across the borders of Couture, to the North ruled **KING KARL**, to the South **KING GIANNI**, to the East **KING GIORGIO** and to the West **KING RALPH**

One day they were in Scotland **hunting** for **faux fur** and they **glimpsed** the Princess **Kate**. She was all alone. She looked miserable. **Her hair** was a moss I mean **mess**. **Her** clothes did not fit. Their Majesties were entranced by her small, spineless stance.

DONNA KARAN
RALPH
THIERRY MUGLER
Behind Kate's back, the beautiful but rejected! gang-of-four was FUMING. They thought they had the kings in their pockets. Instead, this KISS-OFF Kate slouched along. Being a king's favourite brings forth untold treasure from the eager COURTS of REVLON, LAUDER and other oily, creamy products from a JAR called HOPE

The four were so mad that overnight they began to mutate into Gobblers, a far cry from the pretty pouter-pigeons of yesterday.

Their breasts and lips looked as though they would **explode**.

In desperation, they agreed **to move** their mouths about, smile even, and **speak** to each other.

(Which they had avoided for years.)

"This **princess**," each thought to himself, "will be a **perfect Bride**. She will never hog our **limelight**, she will never take away from our **glory** and for a change, when we lead her up and down the aisle, we shall look **tall**. As tall as the Grand Hubert."

"She won't cover our faces with hideous greasy lipstick kisses. The other **ROYAL PAINS** can be bridesmaids. The peasants and the fashion editors will never know the **difference**..."

COMME DES GARCONS

"Furthermore," each thought with glee, "This little creature will get out of bed for **less** than HK$75,000 (U.S $10,000) because she looks like she's always getting out of **bed**. And that's a bonus." Thus, each set out to unlock the heart of Kate.

But Soft!
The Princess Kate was **spoken for**. The Regent **Bergé** had already **offered** her to the Blessed Innocent Saint Laurent; and the Puritan **Calvinist** had marky-marked her in his own image

And defrocked her

Perhaps that is why the Princess Kate is **doomed** to **gloom**.
And why the High and Mighty Masters of Fashion must carry on searching for queens

And why the Princess Claudia may wind up reigning over Monte Carlo; and the Lady Naomi may yet be obliged to **sing** for her supper on MTV and earn millions of dollars;

and why the Princess Linda must reinvent her hair yet again, shave it off and **add** a TATTOO and inspire **miles** of media coverage; and the Lady Christy will finally perfect her **frozen sneer** and turn into LOT (of money)

BUT FOR THE MOMENT, EVERYONE **UNDER 20** LIVES HAPPILY EVER AFTER.

Acknowledgements

I thank Prosper and Martine Assouline for publishing a book of drawings; Richard Christenson, the youngest and smartest art director, who asked, "Why don't you do a book, Gladys?"; Ellen Nidy, my editor, who stayed cool when I panicked.

I am indebted to designers, publicists, security guards, fashion insiders and minor celebrities for making life hell during the collections. Without their diligence I would not have gathered so much ridiculous material.

I thank my late parents, E.J. and Marthe Perint, who believed in me long before I was conceived; my husband, Simon Palmer, who has to live with me; my sons Tim and Barnaby Palmer who learned the meaning of Mummy's on Deadline. Apologies to the dachshunds, frequently covered in coats of flourescent paint, glitter glue and oil pastels.

My appreciation to Richard Stephens and his daughter Elisa, owners of the Academy of Art College in San Francisco, who hired me to run a fashion department and never complained that I was elsewhere in January, February, March, July, September and October.

Lifelong thanks to the late Muriel Pemberton of St. Martin's School of Art in London who taught me the rules and how to break them. Had she lived to see the virtual revolution, she would have pointed out, "Man can draw; a mouse can't."